Homo Poeticus

BY DANILO KIŠ

Garden, Ashes

A Tomb for Boris Davidovich

The Encyclopedia of the Dead

Hourglass

Homo Poeticus

HOMO POETICUS

Essays and Interviews

DANILO KIŠ

Edited and with an
Introduction by
Susan Sontag

Farrar • Straus • Giroux / New York

The editor gratefully acknowledges permission to reprint material from the following previously published sources: *Aristotle*, edited by Richard McKeon. Copyright © 1992 by Richard McKeon. Reprinted by permission of Oxford University Press (UK). "Free Thought and Official Propaganda," from *The Will to Doubt* by Bertrand Russell. Copyright © 1958 by the Philosophical Library. Reprinted by permission of Philosophical Library, Inc. "The Urge to Self-Destruction," from *The Heel of Achilles: Essays 1968–1973* by Arthur Koestler. Copyright © 1974 by Arthur Koestler. Reprinted by permission of Random House, Inc. *Language* by Otto Jespersen. Copyright © 1964 by Otto Jespersen. Reprinted by permission of HarperCollins Publishers (UK). *Theory of Prose* by Victor Shklovsky. Copyright © 1990 by Viktor Shklovsky. Reprinted by permission of Dalkey Archive Press. "The Argentine Writer and Tradition," from *Labyrinths* by Jorge Luis Borges. Copyright © 1962, 1964 by New Directions. Reprinted by permission of New Directions Publishing Corp. "Salon 1846," from *Selected Writings on Art and Artists* by Charles Baudelaire, translated by P. E. Charvet. Copyright © 1972 by P. E. Charvet. Reprinted by permission of Penguin Books Ltd. (UK). *Lolita* by Vladimir Nabokov. Copyright © 1955 by Vladimir Nabokov. Reprinted by permission of Random House, Inc.

"Introduction to *The Anatomy Lesson*" and "Ironic Lyricism" were originally published in *Formations*, volume 2, number 1 (Spring 1985), and volume 5, number 2 (Fall 1989), respectively. "Ironic Lyricism" was originally titled "An Interview with Danilo Kiš." They are reprinted here by permission of Yale University Press. "Censorship/Self-Censorship" was originally published in the November 3, 1985, issue of *The New York Times Book Review* as "The State, the Imagination, and the Censored I," and is reprinted here by permission of The New York Times Company.

Library of Congress Cataloging-in-Publication Data
Kiš, Danilo, 1935–1989.
Homo poeticus : essays and interviews / Danilo Kiš ; edited and
with an Introduction by Susan Sontag.
p.   cm.
1. Kiš, Danilo, 1935–1989—Translations into English.   2. Kiš,
Danilo, 1935–1989—Interviews.   3. Authors, Serbian—20th century—
Interviews.   I. Sontag, Susan.   II. Title.
PG1419.21.I8H66   1995   891.8'245—dc20   94-32499 CIP

Contents

Essays

Interviews

Translators and Interviewers

Introduction

The death of Danilo Kiš on October 15, 1989, at the age of fifty-four, wrenchingly cut short one of the most important journeys in literature made by any writer during the second half of the twentieth century. Born on the rim of the Yugoslav cauldron (in Subotica, near the frontier with Hungary) a few years before the Second World War to a Hungarian Jewish father (Kiš is a Hungarian name), who perished in Auschwitz, and a Serb Orthodox mother from rural Montenegro, raised mostly in Hungary and in Montenegro, a graduate in literature of the university in Belgrade, where he made his debut as a writer, eventually a part-time expatriate, doing some teaching in France, and finally a full-time one, in Paris, where he lived his last ten years, Kiš had a life span that matched, from start to finish, what might have been thought the worst the century had to offer his part of Europe: Nazi conquest and the genocide of the Jews, followed by Soviet takeover.

1989, the year Kiš died of cancer, was of course the

annus mirabilis in which Soviet-style totalitarian rule ended in Central Europe. By mid-October, the collapse of what had seemed immutable was clearly underway; three weeks later, the Berlin Wall was torn down. It is comforting to think that he died knowing only the good news. Happily—it is the only thing about his premature death which gives some consolation—he didn't live to see the collapse of the multi-confessional, multi-ethnic state of which he was a citizen (his "mixed" origin made Kiš very much a Yugoslav), and the return on European soil, in his own country, of concentration camps and genocide. An ardent foe of nationalist vanities, he would have loathed Serb ethnic fascism even more than he loathed the neo-Bolshevik official culture of the Second Yugoslavia it has replaced. It is hard to imagine that, if he were still alive, he could have borne the destruction of Bosnia.

The amount of history, or horror, a writer is obliged to endure does not make him or her a great writer. But geography is destiny. For Kiš there was no retreating from an exalted sense of the writer's place and of the writer's responsibility that, literally, came with the territory. Kiš came from a small country where writers are for better and for worse important, with the most gifted becoming moral, and sometimes even political, legislators. Perhaps more often for worse: it was eminent Belgrade writers who provided the ideological underpinning of the Serbian genocidal project known as "ethnic cleansing." The complicity of most Serb writers and artists not in exile in the current triumph of Greater Serbian imperialism suggests that the anti-nationalist voices, of which Kiš was the bravest and most eloquent, have always been in the minority. Much as by temperament and exquisitely cosmopolitan literary culture he would have preferred a less embattled course, in which literature was kept separate from politics, Kiš was always under attack and therefore, necessarily, on the attack. The first fight was against provincialism. This was not so much the provincialism of a small literature (for the former Yugoslavia produced at least two world-class prose writers, Ivo Andrić and Miroslav Krleža) as of a state-supported, state-rewarded literature. It could be fought simply by his being the utterly independent, artistically ambitious writer he was, almost from the beginning. But worse attacks were to come.

One of those writers who are first of all readers, who prefer dawdling and grazing and blissing out in the Great Library and surrender to their vocation only when the urge to write becomes unbearable, Kiš was not what would be called prolific. In his lifetime he published nine books, seven of them in the fourteen years between 1962, when he was twenty-seven, and 1976, when he was forty-one. First came a pair of short novels, *The Attic* and *Psalm 44* (published in 1962; not yet translated into English). The second book, *Garden, Ashes* (1965), was a novel. The third, *Early Sorrows* (1968, also not yet translated), was a book of stories. The fourth, *Hourglass* (1972), was a novel. The fifth and sixth were two collections of essays, *Po-etika* (1972) and *Po-etika II* (1974). The seventh, *A Tomb for Boris Davidovich* (1976), was a collection of thematically linked stories that his publishers chose to call a novel. He wrote it while an instructor in Serbo-Croatian at the University of Bordeaux, as he'd written *Garden, Ashes* when he taught at Strasbourg.

By this time, Kiš was spending more and more time abroad, though he did not consider himself to be in exile, any more than he would have said he was a "dissident writer": it was too clear to him that writing worthy of the name of literature had to be unofficial. With this seventh book, a suite of fictional case histories of the Stalinist Terror, Kiš's work finally attracted the international attention it deserved. *A Tomb for Boris Davidovich* also attracted a seven-month-long campaign of negative attention back home in Belgrade. The campaign, which reeked of anti-Semitism, centered on an accusation, that the book was a web of plagiarisms from an arcane bibliography, to which Kiš had no choice but to respond. The result was his eighth book, *The Anatomy Lesson* (1978). Defending *A Tomb for Boris Davidovich* against these scurrilous charges, Kiš mounted a full-scale exposition of his literary genealogy (that is, his literary tastes), a post- or proto-modernist poetics of the novel, and a portrait of what a writer's honor could be. During the next ten years, he published only one more book, *The Encyclopedia of the Dead* (1984), a collection of unlinked stories.

The Western European, and eventually North American, acclaim for *A Tomb for Boris Davidovich*—typically confining it within the literature of dissidence from "the other Europe"—had brought about translations of the earlier books into the major foreign languages, and Kiš started to be invited to first-rank literary conferences, to win prizes, and to seem a plausible Nobel candidate. Becoming an internationally famous writer meant becoming a much interviewed writer. Asked to pronounce on literary matters and, invariably, to comment on the infamies back home, he did so with a rueful, always incisive combativeness—he gave splendidly substantive interviews. He was also asked to contribute short pieces to newspapers and magazines—treating no literary solicitation as ever less than an occasion for intensity. Recalling that Kiš published only one book of fiction in the last decade of his life, one can't but regret that he gave as many interviews, wrote as many essays and prefaces, as he did. A poet in prose as well as a prince of indignation, Kiš surely was not best employed in these discursive forms. No great writer of fiction is. And unlike Italo Calvino and Thomas Bernhard, who were also lost to literature in the late 1980s, Kiš had probably not yet done the best of what he was capable in fiction. But the novels and stories he did write still assure him a place alongside these two somewhat senior, far more prolific contemporaries— which is to say that Kiš is one of the handful of incontestably major writers of the second half of the century.

Kiš had a complicated literary genealogy, which he was undoubtedly simplifying when he declared himself, as he often did, a child of Borges and of Bruno Schulz. But to marry the cosmopolitan Argentine to the immured small-town Polish Jew sounds the right note. Most obviously, he was claiming foreign relatives over his descendance from his native Serbo-Croatian literary family. Specifically, by yoking together the serenely, speculatively erudite Borges and the inward-looking, hyperdescriptive Schulz, he was pointing to the principal double strand in his own work. Odd mixtures were very much to Kiš's taste. His "mixed" literary methods—most fully realized in *Hourglass* (historical fiction) and *A Tomb for Boris Davidovich* (fictional history)—gave him exactly the right freedoms to advance the cause of both truth and art. Finally: one can, in literature, choose one's own parents. But nobody obliges a writer to declare his or her parentage. Kiš, however, had to proclaim his. Like every writer who is a great reader, he was an inveterate enthusiast about the work of others. His talent for admiration also made him an extremely collegial writer, which he expressed best in his numerous translations of contemporary writers he undertook from French, Hungarian, Russian, and English into Serbo-Croatian. In expatriation he was still really back home, in his head and in all his work— despite his lived estrangement from the literary world of his native country. He had never forsaken them, though they had betrayed him.

When Kiš died in Paris in 1989, the Belgrade press went into national mourning. The renegade star of Yugoslav literature had been extinguished. Safely dead, he could be eulogized by the mediocrities who had always envied him and had engineered his literary excommunication, and who would then proceed—as Yugoslavia fell apart—to become official writers of the new post-Communist, national chauvinist order. Kiš is, of course, admired by everyone who genuinely cares about literature, in Belgrade as elsewhere. The place in the former Yugoslavia where he was and is perhaps most ardently admired is Sarajevo. Literary people there did not exactly ply me with questions about American literature when I went to Sarajevo for the first time in April 1993. But they were extremely impressed that I'd had the privilege of being a friend of Danilo Kiš. In besieged Sarajevo people think a lot about Danilo Kiš. His fervent screed against nationalism, incorporated into *The Anatomy Lesson*, is one of the two prophetic texts—the other is a story by Andrić, "A Letter from 1920"—that one hears most often cited. As secular, multi-ethnic Bosnia—Yugoslavia's Yugoslavia—is crushed under the new imperative of one ethnicity / one state, Kiš is more present than ever. He deserves to be a hero in Sarajevo, whose struggle to survive embodies the honor of Europe.

Unfortunately, the honor of Europe has been lost at Sarajevo. Kiš and like-minded writers who spoke up against nationalism and fomented-from-the-top ethnic hatreds could not save Europe's honor, Europe's better idea. But it is not true that, to paraphrase Auden, a great writer does not make anything happen. At the end of the century, which is the end of many things, literature, too, is besieged. The work of Danilo Kiš preserves the honor of literature.

July 1994

A Note about This Book

In 1990, the year after Danilo Kiš died, three volumes of his essays, short articles, early poems, and interviews were assembled by his ex-wife, Mirjana Miočinović. (Sign of bygone times, 1990 being the last full year of the former Yugoslavia's existence: two were brought out by a Sarajevo publisher, one by a publisher in Belgrade.) This book, whose choice of texts is mine, obviously does not correspond to any of these posthumous volumes. It is a selection from the material they contain as well as from *The Anatomy Lesson* (1978), to which I have added two uncollected interviews, and, by way of a prologue, a poignantly laconic autobiographical sketch Kiš wrote for a small Belgrade magazine. I continue to hope that one day all of *The Anatomy Lesson* will be thought worth bringing into English, as it has been in French. The argument against translating the whole book is that it presumes too much detailed knowledge of *A Tomb for Boris Davidovich*, Kiš's masterwork of simulated historical narratives which had come under attack by a cabal of influential, "official" Belgrade writers, as Kiš's frequently *ad hominem* counterattack presumes more interest in a faraway literary scene than can be asked of provincial, English-language readers. I don't agree. But, for the time being, this book deposits into English at least some of the best passages of *The Anatomy Lesson*, a strenuous poetics of prose fiction as well as a model exercise of justified rage. A few of Kiš's interviews and essays had already appeared in English, mostly in literary quarterlies. The texts I did not know I read in the versions in French done by Pascale Delpech, Kiš's regular French translator, the companion of his last decade, and his literary co-executor. I am extremely grateful to Pascale Delpech and Mirjana Miočinović for giving their support to this book—I can't believe they do not regret its incompleteness, as I do— and also want to thank Michael Henry Heim for some last-minute, useful suggestions about my selection.

S.S.

Homo Poeticus

Birth Certificate
(A Short Autobiography)

My father came into the world in western Hungary and was educated at the school of commerce in the native city of a certain Mr. Virág, who, by the grace of Mr. Joyce, eventually became the famous Leopold Bloom. I believe it was the liberal policy of Franz Josef II together with a desire for integration that led my grandfather to Magyarize the surname of his underage son, though many details of the family chronicle will remain forever obscure: in 1944 my father and all our relatives were taken off to Auschwitz, and almost none returned.

Among my mother's ancestors is a legendary Montenegrin hero who learned to read and write at the age of fifty, thereby adding the glory of the pen to the glory of the sword, and an "Amazon" who took revenge on a Turkish despot by cutting off his head. The ethnographic rarity I represent will die out with me.

In 1939, when I was four and anti-Jewish laws were being promulgated in Hungary, my parents had me baptized in the Orthodox faith at the Church of the Assumption in Novi Sad. It saved my life. Until the age of thirteen, I lived in my father's native region in Hungary, to which we fled in 1942, following the Novi Sad massacre. I worked as a servant for rich peasants, and in school I went to catechism and Catholic Bible study. The "troubling strangeness" that Freud calls *Heimlichkeit* would be my basic literary and metaphysical stimulus. At the age of nine I wrote my first poems, in Hungarian; one was about hunger, the other was a love poem par excellence.

From my mother I inherited a propensity for telling tales with a mixture of fact and legend; from my father—pathos and irony. My relationship to literature has also been affected by the fact that my father was the author of an international timetable, an entire cosmopolitan and literary legacy in itself.

My mother was a reader of novels until the age of twenty, when she realized, not without regret, that they were "fabrications," and rejected them for good. Her aversion to "pure fabrication" is latent in me as well.

In 1947 we were repatriated by the Red Cross to Montenegro, the home of my uncle, a well-known historian and a biographer of and commentator on Njegoš.* Immediately after we arrived, I took the art-school entrance examination. (The admissions committee included Petar Lubarda and Milo Milunović.) The bust of Voltaire we were asked to draw—a plaster cast of Houdon's statue—reminded me of an elderly German woman I knew in

---

* Petar Petrović Njegoš (1813–51), Prince-Bishop of Montenegro and author of *The Mountain Wreath*, a long philosophical poem considered one of the masterworks of Serb literature.

Novi Sad, and that is how I drew him. I was accepted nonetheless, probably on the basis of other work. I had to wait a year or two until I had the necessary academic preparation. During that time I decided to complete the Gymnasium program instead.

For two years I studied violin at the local music school, where I was taught by Simonuti Senior, whom we called "Paganini" not only for his appearance but for his love of vibrato. Just as I reached the second position, the music school moved to Kotor. I went on playing by ear, specializing in Gypsy music, Hungarian romances, and—at school dances—the tango and "English" waltzes.

At the Gymnasium I continued to write poetry. I also translated Hungarian, Russian, and French poets, primarily as a stylistic and linguistic exercise: I was training to be a poet, learning the craft of literature. We were taught Russian by White Army officers, émigrés from the twenties who substituted for absent teachers and were equally at home in mathematics, physics, chemistry, French, and Latin.

From the Gymnasium I entered the University of Belgrade, where I was the first student to graduate from the newly created Department of Comparative Literature.

As an instructor in Serbo-Croatian language and literature I have taught at Strasbourg, Bordeaux, and Lille: for the last few years I have been living in Paris, in the tenth arrondissement, and am not at all homesick. At times I wake up not knowing where I am; I hear my compatriots calling to one another and an accordion blaring from a cassette player in a car parked beneath my window.

1983

Introduction to
The Anatomy Lesson

The unprecedented witch-hunt surrounding *A Tomb for Boris Davidovich* and its author has died down like a provincial carnival: the windows are dark, the curtains drawn, the dogs quiet, the marketplace strewn with newsprint, the last evidence of that Walpurgis Night, that (literary) witches' sabbath.

And since literary historians may someday try to make sense of it all ("the biggest postwar literary scandal in the country," according to the press) by piling high the yellowed newspapers and piecing together what actually went on during this period of literary bedlam, I should like to provide them with a few facts that may be of interest and help them to make their way in the darkness.

For despite the prodigious amounts of ink spilled and bile secreted, the literary investigators of the future will find it hard to get their bearings: most of the action took place behind the scenes in our literary "salons" and clubs, our literary bar and grill, and the press coverage was mostly of the sensation-mongering variety; in other words, stupid.

Yet, were it not for the yellow press and the failed writers-turned-reporters who set the tone, I might never have written this book; I might have had no need to write it because I would have been able to say all I had to say —or most of it—in the newspapers. In fact, I did write some articles at the time (exposing a few misunderstandings and unclear points), but was unable to have them published because of the alleged objectivity of our literary and non-literary press (whose editors held that as an interested party I had no right to speak out on matters of the utmost concern to me), or withdrew them myself, realizing that papers with a large circulation would have selected only the most sensational items (as they had done with some earlier pieces of mine), thus stripping the whole of all logic and argumentative power.

The witch-hunt was at its height for a period of seven months (from September 1976 to March 1977—now in the open, now behind the scenes), and the polemical bonfire that burst forth on the pages of our newspapers lit up the face of our provincial literary scene. But only for a moment. Once the flames threatened to singe the troublemakers intriguing in the darkness, they pulled back and hid behind their institutions and their lies, denying the public, semi-public, and secret allegations of the hour before, happy to escape with second-degree burns. I, however, unable to speak at the time, vowed to follow their writings, subject them to a "close reading," as they say in English, and clear things up—that is, demonstrate on the basis of cogent, instructive examples that they were ill equipped both morally and literarily to pass judgment on books of any kind. I reserve this fun and games for the second part of the book; in the first I shall touch on *A Tomb for Boris Davidovich* itself—its genesis, its sources, and certain theoretical assumptions on which it is based. As the use of paraliterary and documentary materials for literary purposes is a well-known device in modern literature—it has been one of the dominant devices since Flaubert—I shall for pedagogical reasons cite a number of instructive texts.

Given the present state of our literary criticism, a state that shows no promise of improvement, writers are duty-bound to speak out about their texts from a theoretical perspective. In the last analysis, everything that happens to writers—bad or good—forms a part of their literary destiny (and they have no other). *Tout est à aboutir à un livre,* says Mallarmé. Everything in the world exists to be turned into a book.

Once I hit upon the idea not only of demonstrating certain principles underlying *A Tomb for Boris Davidovich* but also of making an anatomical incision into the moral and political heart of *cosa nostra* and Jeremićian* criticism, the aesthetic heart of our literary banditry, I beheld Rembrandt's *The Anatomy Lesson of Dr. Nicolaes Tulp* in my mind's eye as a visual metaphor of the procedure and as the dust cover of the future book. After some hesitation I opted for this *Anatomy Lesson* in the Mauritshuis (The Hague), showing Dr. Tulp and his pupils, instead of the later one, *The Anatomy Lesson of Dr. Deyman* in the Rijksmuseum (Amsterdam), dating from 1656, which I actually

---

* Dragan Jeremić (1925–86), the critic who led the campaign against *A Tomb for Boris Davidovich.*

find more attractive as a painting and illustration of the theme by virtue of its palette, its fate (it withstood the test of fire), its fragmentary nature, and its masterly execution, and while it lacks the facility, the perfection of Dr. Tulp's *Anatomy Lesson*, it renders with masterly ease—as a demonstration of mastery—the bloody entrails of the corpse and the hand holding the scalpel, the hand of Dr. Johann Deyman, which, though in the background, dominates the painting, because the hand holding the glittering, razor-sharp scalpel is likewise the hand of the master, the hand of the man who placed the scalpel into it, painting it with a single stroke of the brush like a single stroke of the bistoury. And even though I later abandoned this illustration in favor of the other, the hand holding the scalpel lingered in my thoughts, and in my mind the shiny steel blade passed into the hands of Dr. Tulp, who as a result of my conflation now holds both the surgeon's knife and the surgeon's scissors! The sole reason I rejected the second canvas in favor of the first was that the first was a public lesson and the body on the operating table a common corpse, as colorless as the body of a drowned man, sterile, sterilized, totally worthless except as an object for demonstrating the symptoms of a pathological state and needing no *brasero* to dispel the stench of decay with the scent of its burning herbs.

Dr. Tulp has used his forceps to separate the muscle fibers of the open wound in the left forearm and is showing his pupils the skein of muscles and tendons, arteries and veins through which blood has ceased to flow, showing it all with the calm and composure of a man who knows that the human body—apart from its spiritual functions, apart from the soul and the ethical component—is nothing but a digestion machine, a gut bucket, a bundle of intestines and nerves, a mass of veins and flesh, like the skinned ox (in the Louvre) that Rembrandt painted some twenty-three years later: a great hunk of meat hung upside down. The doctor's left hand—thumb pressing forefinger, the contact of the epidermis on the fleshy fingertips where the mere brush of a butterfly's wing or a flower's pollen can be felt, delicate, all but non-existent, like a breath, like the fine film that covers an apple and that the French call *brume des cloches*, bell mist —the doctor's upraised living hand attracts more attention on the part of some of the students than the lifeless fore-arm and bared tendons, as if the tightly pressed fingers were about to discharge an electric spark, the incarnation of the soul, the emanation of vitality in contrast to the cadaver's dead sinews, a moral lesson. What vibrates like an emanation between the fingers of Dr. Nicolaes Pietersz Tulp—that spark of knowledge and experience about to burst forth like an electric discharge between two pieces of alabaster charged with a mass of electrons (the students feel that the empirical knowledge of the surgeon's fingers is going to inspire them like the Holy Sacrament), that experience of all previous (anatomical) knowledge—includes the lesson of Dr. Sebastian Egbertsz, just as Rembrandt found "a model and precursor" in *The Anatomy Lesson of Dr. Sebastian Egbertsz* painted by Thomas de Keyser, which features at its core a human skeleton not devoid of metaphysical meaning. Or aesthetic meaning: the message that we divine is inherently present in Rembrandt, an echo of the classical, Aristotelian "aesthetic of ugliness": "Though the objects themselves may be painful to see, we delight to view the most realistic representations of them in art, the forms for example of the lowest animals and of dead bodies.''*

One of the doctor's pupils—or his assistant, the man standing closest to him—is holding a book, a manual of some sort, a textbook of histology, perhaps. To the right of the doctor is a folded sheet of paper. There is no room for improvisation: documents, involvement in the world, anthropometrical skill, the history and results of previous anatomical investigation—it is all there in spirit and logos; the spirit of science prevails, the bibliography is in place, the sum of past experience, from the Pythagorean Alcmeon (who examined anthropoids and speculated on the functions of the human body more or less *per analogiam*), from Galen to Mundinus and Leonardo da Vinci (who is thus related to Rembrandt's *Lesson* twice over), and from Leonardo to the *De humani corporis fabrica* (1543) of Vesalius, from Vesalius to Varolio and Fabricius of Acquapendente, whose work on the arteries and blood vessels Dr. Tulp undoubtedly knew.

The world was not born yesterday. We know—we can see—that this is not the first anatomy lesson under the sun. Yet there are still new truths to be discovered by observation, dissection, and vivisection, by practice and through the sum of experience available to us.

The lesson may now begin.

* Aristotle, *Poetics*, Chapter IV. The "aesthetic of ugliness" we find here in Aristotle receives absolute status in the nineteenth century in the works of Rosenkranz: the ugly is beautiful. [D.K.]

The Gingerbread Heart, or Nationalism

Nationalism is first and foremost *paranoia*, individual and collective paranoia. As collective paranoia it is the product of envy and fear and primarily the result of a loss of individual consciousness; it is thus nothing but a set of individual paranoias raised to the degree of paroxysm. If an individual feels unable to "express himself" within the framework of the social order either because it fails to encourage or stimulate him as an individual or because it constrains him as an individual—in other words, stands in the way of his self-fulfillment—and he feels obliged to seek fulfillment outside his identity or the prevailing social structures, he joins a Masonic-like group dedicated (in appearance, at least) to solving the problems of the age: keeping the nation alive, protecting its prestige, upholding its tradition, safeguarding the national patrimony as represented by its folklore, literature, philosophy, etc. Burdened with this secret, semi-public, or public mission, he becomes a man of action, a tribune of the people, a pseudo-individual; reduced to this dimension, his true dimension, he becomes an individual without individuality, a nationalist, a Cousin Jules.

Sartre's Jules, the *idiot de la famille,* has a single trait: he turns white whenever a certain topic comes up; to wit, the English. His pallor, his tremble, his "mystery"—the ability to turn pale at the mere mention of the English—are his only social identity, the things that give his life meaning, that give him a life. Whatever you do, don't bring up *English* tea in his presence or everyone will start winking at you, making signs, kicking you under the table, because everyone knows Jules is allergic to the English, Jules detests the English (and loves his own, the French); in a word, Jules has an identity, has acquired an identity thanks to *English* tea.

Take this portrait (compatible with all nationalists) to its logical conclusion and the result is clear: as both individual and social being the nationalist is a nobody. Apart from his commitment to the cause, he is nothing. He has abandoned his family, his work (office work, as a rule), literature (if he is a writer), and his social responsibilities because they lose all meaning in the light of his messianism. Needless to say, he is by choice an ascetic, a potential warrior awaiting his hour. Nationalism—to paraphrase Sartre's observation about anti-Semitism—is "a free and total choice, a global attitude one adopts not merely to other nations but to people in general, to history and society; it is at once a passion and a conception of the world." The nationalist is by definition an ignoramus.

Thus, nationalism is the path of least resistance, the easy way out. The nationalist has no problems; he knows—or thinks he knows—his own basic values, his own and therefore his people's, the ethical and political values of the nation to which he belongs. He is interested in no others. Nothing "other" holds any interest for him. Hell is others (other nations, other tribes), people not worth knowing or studying. All the nationalist sees in others is his own image: the image of a nationalist. A comfortable position, as we have said. Fear and envy. A choice, a commitment requiring no effort. The nationalist feels not only that hell is other nations but also that everything not his (Serb, Croat, French . . .) is alien to him.

Nationalism is the ideology of banality. It is a totalitarian ideology. It is also, and not only in the etymological sense, the last ideology and demagogy addressed to the people. And because a writer knows this better than anyone, all writers who proclaim they are writing "of the people and for the people" and claim to subordinate their own voices to the superior interests of the nation are suspect.

Nationalism is also kitsch. In its Serbo-Croat variant, for instance, it is the controversy over the ethnic origin of our gingerbread hearts.* The nationalist typically knows no foreign language (or regional variant of his own), no foreign cultures (they do not concern him), but if as an intellectual he does have access to another language and thus to the cultural heritage of another nation, great or small, he uses it only to draw comparisons— invidious comparisons, naturally. Kitsch and folklore— folk kitsch, if you prefer—are nothing if not nationalism in disguise, a fertile soil for nationalist ideology. The up-

---

* Pastries in the shape of hearts, familiar objects, or famous persons, decorated with colored icing and tiny mirrors, and sold at fairs.

surge of interest in folklore both here and abroad is due less to anthropology than to nationalism.

It is a penchant for the infamous local color when it lies outside the context of art, that is, when it fails to promote artistic truth. But, above all, nationalism is negation, a negative category of the spirit, thriving as it does on repudiation. We are not like them. We are the positive pole; they are the negative pole. Our national and nationalist values have meaning only in relation to the nationalism of others. Yes, we are nationalistic, but they are more so; we cut throats when necessary, they are bloodthirsty; we are drunkards, they are alcoholics. Our history is just only in relation to theirs, our language pure only in relation to theirs.

Nationalism thrives on relativism: it has no universal values, aesthetic or ethical. And because its only values are relative, it is a reactionary ideology. All that counts is outdoing our brother or half brother: no one else need concern us; jumping a little higher than he jumps: no one else matters. Anyone else has the right to catch up with us, even overtake us. We don't care. Nationalism always sets itself attainable goals, attainable because they are modest, modest because they are contemptible. We don't high-jump or shot-put to better our record; we do it to beat them, the others, the only ones who matter, so like us yet so different.

Thus, the nationalist fears no one but his brother. But he fears him with an existential fear, a pathological fear: the victory of the enemy means absolute defeat for the nationalist, the destruction of his very being. Terrified and miserable, he sets no higher goals for himself. Victory over his *chosen* enemy is the only victory. Nationalism depends on despair; it is the ideology of potential victory—guaranteed yet always somehow postponed—and defeat that is never final.

The nationalist fears no one, "no one but God." Yet his is a God made to measure, his double sitting at the next table, his own brother, every bit as impotent as himself, "the pride of the family," a conscious and organized part of the family unit and the nation—a pale Cousin Jim. To be a nationalist, as we have seen, is to be an individual without obligations, "a coward who will not own up to his cowardice, a murderer who represses his homicidal tendencies, cannot quite hold them in check, and dares to kill only in effigy or in the anonymity of a crowd"— the spitting image of Sartre's anti-Semite. And where does his cowardice come from, we wonder. What is the source of his choice, of the rise of nationalism in our time? On the fringe of one or another social movement, wedged between opposing ideologies, denied the possibility of personal revolt, the individual finds himself in a rift, a void: though a social being, he does not participate in social activities; though an individualist, he must disavow his individuality in the name of an ideology. What remains for him but to seek his social identity elsewhere? The nationalist is a frustrated individualist, nationalism the frustrated (collective) expression of his individualism, at once an ideology and anti-ideology.*

Far be it from me to believe that this commentary, this confession will correct the nationalists' arbitrary interpretation and malicious reading of my work. In fact, they

---

* See also Danilo Kiš, *Po-etika, knjiga druga* (Po-Et[h]ics, Book Two) (Belgrade, 1974), 174–81.

will surely proclaim it (orally—the only possibility) a challenge, whereby Bulatović's* destructive machine will be
set in motion and transmit to me by phone his insane
notions about my "spitting on the people." And there is
nothing I can do about it, because the way he reads and
interprets literature follows logically from the kind of psychological, irrational, paranoid instability that sees phan-
toms everywhere, the kind of psychological and moral
degeneracy that reduces everything to the common denominator of *for us* versus *against us*, the kind of murky
consciousness that creates spiritual autos-da-fé at all times
and places and trumpets its "I am everywhere," as a way
of notifying all and sundry that it sees ghosts just as drunkards see mice.

When I brought up Cousin Jules in the context of nationalism during the interview, I did not mean it as a
metaphor "to befuddle the peasantry." I merely wished
to invoke Sartre's familiar and striking example of the psychological consequences attendant upon this paranoid
state of mind, these hallucinations. Similarly, there was no
hidden allusion to any particular Yugoslav author in my
assertion that when writers use (anachronistic) nationalist
slogans they usually do so for demagogic purposes and that
local color ("when it fails to promote artistic truth") is
likewise more often than not a mere component of literary demagogy.

As for "gingerbread hearts"—whose ethnic origins
were recently the subject of venomous debate in the col-
umns of both the Belgrade and the Zagreb press and

---

* Miodrag Bulatović (1930–91), Serb novelist. Several of his works have appeared
in English.

which thus became a symbol of the tawdry, fairground basis for nationalist consciousness with its souvenir mythologems of pastry dough and icing—I first saw them at the Baksa fair (that is, in Hungary) when I was nine. In Hungary they were all red, white, and green (*piros-fehér-zöld, ez a magyar föld,* red, white, and green is our Magyar land), but just as stereotypically national as ours, their icing rosettes and spun-sugar lace surrounding tiny pictures of hussars in authentic red dolmans or red-cheeked czardas dancers in pearl diadems, green blouses, white skirts and petticoats, and blood-red boots decorated with tulips—all purely national down to the last pleat. And if at the time—especially then, in May 1944—you had asked any member of the festive throng milling about the stands, any of the farmhands or urban toughs swarming through the stalls, if you had risked the sacrilege of questioning the national authenticity of the gingerbread heart, they would have been ready not only to swear by Kazinczy, Kossuth, or Petöfi that it had been Hungarian for a thousand years but also to hack out your own overinquisitive, doubting heart right there in public.

Which is why the issue raised so dramatically in the press as central to our national identity—the issue of whether a photograph of a gingerbread heart shown in the papers had been taken here in Serbia at Paraćin or across the river in Croatia at Varaždin—struck me then and strikes me now as preposterous, unworthy of the breath or ink wasted on it (never mind the bile and blood), an issue totally devoid of interest (except perhaps for ethnologists) and in the given context as hollow as the gingerbread heart and—as the French say—made of the same flour.

During the years when one's views of the world take shape, when myths and prejudices make their mark on one's soul, when one's mythic and social character comes into being, I had the good (or bad) fortune to learn the hard way about the relativity of all myths, beginning with those that date from early childhood: that the boys in my street, Bem Street, were the strongest and made the best friends; that they fought only in self-defense or to wreak vengeance; that their territory was sacred and inviolable, a sacred *terra nostrana* where trespassing was forbidden and therefore punishable (a motif that would later move me in Ferenc Molnár's novel *The Paul Street Boys*). As luck would have it, I was early obliged (like a literary character whose all-powerful creator enjoyed playing games with his destiny) to take a different "point of view" because not only did I learn—horrors!—that we would be moving from Bem Street to Greek School Street or—horror of horrors!—from Louis Barthou Street all the way to Telep, home of the most hardened criminals and murderers, but I soon realized that in this cruel *Homo ludens* game (which eventually found its "ideological" and psychological metathesis, its mythological parable in William Golding's novel *Lord of the Flies*), in this pubescent brand of totalitarianism, concepts tend to become relative and convictions and prejudices, raised to the level of absolute moral categories and principles, crumble and vanish before our eyes as soon as we look at them *from the other side* of the wall or border, from the other side of the barricade built by the cruel, never-ending adolescent imperialism and chauvinism that thrives on the fringes of big cities, in the poor sections of small towns, in the shadow of brickyards and shanties, where territorial integrity is defended "to the last drop of blood" and a community bounded

by the ideological border of a street or village is governed
by legends handed down from generation to generation,
a community forged and reinforced by the memory of
heroic exploits, by the intermingling of blood squeezed
from fingertips, solemn oaths à la David, by codes and
shibboleths, whistle blasts replacing bugles and making
hearts leap with joy, ritual tests of strength and courage,
secret names and nicknames (from penny dreadfuls), the
discovery of the mysteries of the body and sex, the cul-
tivation of legends that, as children grow into adults, fade
into nostalgic memories of childhood.

This dim awareness of the relativity of things, the
crumbling of a belief in the existence of a single and
unique constant, constituted the horror of my childhood
years, a horror that took the place of my early anxieties.
Here I was, obliged for unfathomable reasons to leave
Bem Street and the established order of a pubescent kingdom ruled by a cruel yet just *Volksdeutscher* armed with a
knife and a pair of binoculars, a realm where everyone in
the labyrinth of air-raid shelters and freshly dug trenches
(intended for a different ritual but bloodier and crueler
only in its consequences) had a clear-cut place, clear-cut
duties and obligations, and the conviction that he was
living in the best of all possible worlds.

Once my first fear of being found out, exposed, of being cruelly punished, had subsided, I realized with astonishment verging on incredulity that here, too, in this new
neighborhood the same laws held sway, the same myths
of community / strength / fidelity, the same hatred of the
"enemy," whose territory began three streets away, a
territory inhabited exclusively by criminals, good-for-
nothings, blasphemers and thieves, the sons of alcoholics,
bandits, and madmen, arsonists and murderers all, armed

with bicycle chains, knives, and brass knuckles, smashers of windows, seducers of little girls, fornicators, and all-round scoundrels, whom it was our duty to destroy in the name of *our* chivalric tradition, *our* brand of fair play. (It was only later that the list of mortal sins came to include the most shameful of all, that of being circumcised, of being a *büdös zsidó*, a dirty Jew, a discovery that in the world of childhood was merely the reflex of the cruel events culminating in the bloody massacre of January 1942, the infamous "cold days" of Novi Sad, when the cruel children's game would end tragically for so many beneath the ice of the Danube.)

The repeated, sudden, incomprehensible uprootings, the changes of residence and address—what I could not see was that my father hoped that by moving from one place to another he could escape his destiny or that in addition to the objective component there lurked behind it all a latent anxiety neurosis endemic to the Jewish intelligentsia of Central Europe—soon made me very much aware of the relativity of myths, and not just pubescent ones. Later, living in the Hungarian countryside as a farmhand and village orphan yet with the world view and habits of a city boy (that is, aware of not belonging, of being out of my element), I soon, both at school and among the peasant families who took me in out of curiosity, absorbed various local Hungarian myths and commonplaces of oral tradition: counting rhymes, proverbs, sayings. "Hungarians are the most hospitable people in the world," the hardest working, the most religious; Hungarian soldiers are the most valiant and loyal; *Talpra magyar, hí a haza!* (Arise, O Magyar, your country calls!); the Hungarian plain is the most beautiful vista in the world (according to objective witnesses, foreign travelers), mountains being harsh and inhospitable; "Who says the puszta is not beautiful?" (Petöfi); it is foreigners who have tried to ruin Hungary (*Nem, nem, soha!* No, no, never!), but now (my children!) our land is as great and beautiful as it was in the days of King Stephen, King István, "a posy on God's hat," for the God of the Hungarians wears the hat of a *csikós*, a puszta cowboy, and needless to say His hat is adorned with Hungarian wildflowers, flowers known to no other country, like the *búzavirág* (cornflower), the *gyöngyvirág* (lily of the valley), the *bazsalikom* (basil), the *bazsarózsa* (peony): *Ha a föld Isten kalapja, hazánk a bokréta rajta* (If the earth is God's hat, our country is the posy on it); Hungarian history is the bloodiest, the most heroic, the most just; Hungarian rulers are the noblest and most civilized, though constantly betrayed by perfidious allies; Hungary was the rampart that held back the Turkish invaders; Hungarian is the most beautiful language on earth (all others pale in shame beside it), which is clear from its fixed epithet *szép: a szép magyar nyelv*, "the *beautiful* Hungarian language"; Hungarian literature is the finest, Hungarian horses are the fleetest, Hungarian heroes the bravest; the regiments of Hungarian hussars fighting in Stalingrad are fiercer than the rest because in Stalingrad the Hungarian soldier, the *honvéd* (literally, "homeland defender"), is defending his homeland. *Esik esö ázik, magyar baka fázik* (It is raining, the Hungarian private is soaked and freezing) and *Ugye gondolsz néha rám, csillagfényes éjszakán* . . . (Do you sometimes think of me in the starry night?), Katalin Karady's tearjerker coming over the schoolmistress's radio, and *Tudom, hogy vársz* (I know you're waiting for me), though objectively the latter had ceased to be anything but a requiem for hundreds and thousands of *honvéd*s, senseless victims of "a hero's death" on the snow-covered steppes of faraway Russia . . .

I accepted it all with the trust and innocence of a child in spite of certain doubts, vague notions, in spite of my experience and a presentiment that this was no place for me, for us, that we were here only for the interim, that we were war refugees, foreigners, exiles living the hard life of exile in the shadow of death. In *Garden, Ashes* I dealt with it all as fiction: my preconscious awareness of a hereditary curse and my long juvenile religious crises and sufferings brought on by the Catholic ritual, the Children's Catechism, the Children's Bible, *Gyermekszívek hódolata* (The Homage of Children's Hearts), the harmonium as played by the schoolmistress, Mass, First Communion (from which I was excluded), bell ringing at the village church, the fear of divine retribution. All the lyrical pathos of the Catholic Church—the servers in satin and lace ringing handbells and carrying on a solemn, Latin dialogue with the village priest (the *plébános*), the congregation chanting, the harmonium exalting the soul to Heaven—seemed to me no more than a pretext for penitence and torment, and when the schoolmistress (clearly wishing to secure the indulgence of the village fascists for us) appointed me chief carol singer and I went from house to house with my schoolmates dressed in floppy linen peasant trousers and vest and the hat and whip of a *csikós* and carrying the manger with cloth-and-wood figures of the newborn babe and the Three Magi, I was still sick at heart, because even as I stood singing "Shepherds, Arise" on the village doorsteps I knew I was there only thanks to the schoolmistress's indulgence and intervention.

At home with my mother, on the other hand, I spent the long winter evenings with another legend and another God, less stern, less cruel, almost pagan, and I said the

Lord's Prayer in Church Slavonic. That Lord's Prayer was my first (oral) translation and my first precocious awareness of both the parallels *inter nobilissimas Europae linguas* and my first intimation of the force of *zaum'*, the "transrational language" of the Russian futurists, and of what Wundt calls *Lautbilder*, phonetic images.

Then, from 1947 on, in Cetinje, Montenegro—in the home of my maternal grandfather, who answered to the biblical name of Jacob—I, as "man of the house," carried in the Yule log. My aunt would kneel and cross herself on the straw-covered floor, blessing me with sugar and nuts while pronouncing the magic words *Da priidet tsarstvie Tvoe* (Thy kingdom come) in Church Slavonic, to which, by way of conjuring fate and appeasing the evil spirits, she added ritualistic inventions of her own like *Anatematenate, ćorilo* (Anathemauponyou, one-eyed), unaware that the Russian poet Kruchenykh had done so long before her in his transrational poem *"Dyr bul shchyl"* and the Prophet Isaiah long before him (*Sav la-sav, sav la-sav / Kav la-kav, kav la-kav / Zeer sham, zeer sham*), and as the sugar crunched under our feet, the candle flames flickered, and the icon lamp crackled beneath St. Michael the Archangel, our holy patron and protector or, rather, the pagan tutelary deity of the house, the *domovoi* covered with soot, gilt, and fly droppings, we would toast the occasion with wine or brandy: *Khristos se rodi—Voistinu se rodi* (Christ is born—Verily He is born). *Dyr bul shchyl.*

My (maternal) grandfather wrote poems in decasyllabic verse.* (I once jotted down two or three of them and

---

* The ten-syllable or decasyllabic line is the standard line of South Slav heroic poetry, which was collected and published by the language reformer Vuk Karadžić (1787–1864).

dreamed of collecting folk poetry like Vuk Karadžić.)
Turkish heads soared through the air like ears of corn (my
grandfather had actually fought at Taraboš in 1912–13),
horses neighed as in Homer, Christians pursued the infi-
dels "as far as Scutari and farther," there was great feasting
in honor of the victory, pagan celebrations at which great
quantities of smoked ham and Njeguš cheese were washed
down with brandy from Dobrsko Selo and red wine from
Crmnica and the Turkish heads were flung at the feet of
the glorious master (Nicholas I), etc. Everyone was a hero,
each more intrepid than the last, and Montenegro and the
seven hills had never been taken by the Turks, never sur-
rendered. I could have sworn I had heard them all
before—the poems, the stories from my school textbook
(Jagoš Jovanović's *History of Montenegro*), the same heroic
exploits with the same moral, the same Homeric exaggeration; I could have sworn I had picked the blood-
soaked peonies of Kosovo in other patriotic odes in
another language under the name of *bazsarózsa*.* And by
the time I left Cetinje at the ripe old age of eighteen, I
had come to the realization, largely thanks to my readings
(Cecil Roth and later Albert Memmi, Elie Wiesel, Max
Brod, Franz Kafka [the diaries], Arthur Koestler, etc.), that
the Jewish myth of the "chosen people" comes from just
another national—Old Testament and Talmudic—mythology writ large and that Talmudic precepts and Hasidic
legends are essentially no different from Vuk's proverbs or
Christian, Greco-Roman, Byzantine, and ancient Indian
precepts and legends.

---

* Just as I was to find them under the name of *coquelicots* in French textbooks and
readers, not only in the works of third-rate *cocorico* poets but in Victor Hugo as well.
[D.K.]

Thus, an awareness of the relativity of all national myths (a subject that deserves a volume of its own) ripened in me spontaneously, like a fruit, and although I had never clearly formulated the idea that began to obsess me—that it would be interesting to read up on how all this was treated in, say, Turkish or German or Italian history books—when at length I came across it in someone else ("Napoleon's campaigns of 1813 and 1814, for instance, might be studied in the *Moniteur*, leading up to the surprise which Parisians felt when they saw the Allies arriving under the walls of Paris after they had [according to the official bulletins] been beaten by Napoleon in every battle"*) nearly word for word as I had carried it about with me, I recognized it as something that had in fact obsessed me since childhood.

I am convinced that history taught as Bertrand Russell would have it taught would have far-reaching implications, that a theory of historical relativity would have repercussions no less fundamental than Einstein's theory of relativity, that it could resolve countless misunderstandings and prevent countless tragic blunders without disturbing the constant (which in a different context Stanislav Vinaver† called the H constant by analogy with Planck's theory of discrete value in quantum mechanics), the discrete constant of national characteristics. On the contrary!

Granted, it is a utopian project and would lead to new misunderstandings: each party would demand the right to interpret the texts of the others, because each of us chooses the myths that we wish to believe and that help us to live. "Identification with the group always involves

---

* Bertrand Russell, *Let the People Think* (London, 1941), 40.
† Stanislav Vinaver (1891–1955), Serb poet, essayist, and translator.

a sacrifice of the individual's critical faculties, and an en-
hancement of his emotional potential by a kind of group-
resonance or positive feedback . . . All this points to the
conclusion that the predicament of man is not caused by
the aggressivity of the individual, but by the dialectics of
group-formation; by man's irresistible urge to identify
with the group and espouse its beliefs enthusiastically and
uncritically . . . Without words there would be no
poetry—and no war. Language is the main source of our
superiority over brother animal—and, in view of its ex-
plosive potentials, the main threat to our survival . . . Each
language acts as a powerful cohesive force within the
group and as an equally powerful divisive force between
groups."* So back we are at the beginning again, for in
the beginning was the Word.

Rivarol's *Discours sur l'universalité de la langue française*
(1784), that "ardent and scintillating apologia for the
French language and national genius," is merely a variant
on "the beautiful Hungarian language" (*a szép magyar
nyelv*), "our sweet mother tongue" (*édes anyanyelvünk*), in
short, on the romantic notion that whatever language *we*
speak is the most beautiful, the most vivid, the most me-
lodious, the most functional, the best adapted to the (noble) human soul; indeed, there is nary a civilized nation
whose literary and philosophical library does not contain
an "ardent and scintillating apologia" for the language and
genius of the nation, a notion that developed not only
with the passage from Latin to the *vulgaris eloquentia* but
also with the wars of liberation and the awakening of

* Arthur Koestler, "The Urge to Self-Destruction," *The Heel of Achilles: Essays
1968–1973* (Random House, 1974), 13–15.

national consciousnesses during the Napoleonic invasions. Apologias for a language of one's own, a language expressive of the national character, would bloom in the romantic period like peonies in the fields of Kosovo, soaked red with the blood of the people.* They are still prevalent—"Writing one's language properly is a form of patriotism."—Lucie Delarue-Mardius (*La Liberté*, 1933)— in the guise of, say, the philological passions of late romanticism or the philological jousts between Zagreb and Belgrade, each of which has its "sweet mother tongue" down on index cards, so alike in structure, so different in aroma, queen bees ready at any moment to stab each other with their poisoned stings, each convinced of the authenticity and purity of her particular healing nectar.† Rome and Byzantium! Schism! "Wars are fought for words. They are man's most deadly weapon."‡

It goes without saying that all attempts to determine the degree of a language's philological and semantic "accuracy," establish a scientific methodology or criteria—a kind of "linguistic chic"—for assessing it on aesthetic or logical grounds (such as vowel frequency or nasalization), substantiate its "purity" with respect to other languages, etc., are as futile as seeking its superiority in the numerical riches of its lexicon, an abundance of synonyms being in fact a sign of a language's "impurity," of its "inauthentic-

---

* According to Serb legend, the peonies that sprang up after the Battle of Kosovo against the Turks (1389) were fed by the blood of fallen Serbs.

† The Serb and Croat institutions charged with safeguarding linguistic purity (and thus analogous in function to the Académie Française and the Academia Española for French and Spanish) are called, respectively, Matica Srpska and Matica Hrvatska, *matica* meaning, literally, "queen bee."

‡ Koestler, "The Urge to Self-Destruction," 14.

ity," since the wealth of parallel synonyms comes mainly from foreign borrowings. The late-romantic misapprehension of one's mother tongue being not only as sweet and healing as nectar but also the most perfect in the world is perhaps a last sweet misapprehension, a last myth, a force for both cohesion and strife among nations and the force on which the frail equilibrium of our (European) linguistic Babylon depends.

And not only European. Domination by language is as old as domination by arms. Sometimes number—numerical superiority—wins out, sometimes spirit (language). In the end, as Eliade has said, the world is nothing but language speaking to us by means of its mode of existence, structures, and rhythms. Language thus understood is just another myth, though it calls for certain new conclusions; namely, that even my "sweet language" is relative (and hence can be spoken of only in terms of subjective categories) and that all I can conclude from the fact that I write solely (and therefore best) in my own language is the self-evident fact that I write solely (and therefore best) in my own language. That is what makes it the sole (and best) language for me.* That and nothing more.

---

* "Gabelentz says that the casual observer has no idea how manifold and how nicely circumscribed grammatical categories can be, even in the seemingly crudest languages . . . P. W. Schmidt says that whoever, from the low culture of the Andamanese, would expect to find their language very simple and poor in expression would be strangely deceived, for its mechanism is highly complicated, with many prefixes and suffixes, which often conceal the root itself. Meinhof mentions the multiplicity of plural formations in African languages. Vilhelm Thomsen, in speaking of the Santhal (Khervarian) language, says that its grammar is capable of expressing a multiplicity of nuances which in other languages must be expressed by clumsy circumlocutions."—Otto Jespersen, *Language* (Norton Library, 1964), 427.

"Our impressions of another nation's language often shift from the linguistic to other

I am constantly aware of the subjectivity of this or that of my thoughts and opinions, constantly aware of the relativity—that is, universality—of my preferences. All around me, all around us—a few hours' journey to the east, west, north, or south—there are thousands of writers bending over pages full of words and caressing or reviling "the most beautiful, the most proud, the most modest, the most bold, the most touching, the most voluptuous, the most chaste, the most noble, the most intimate, the most mad and most wise"* language on earth, the best adapted to the noblest of human souls, the soul of the poet. And if ever these distant (and close) relatives of mine get the blasphemous idea that "language has betrayed them," it is only because their pen has faltered and they have failed to come up with the proper word or turn of phrase, for casting doubt upon their language (the language they write in) would mean ceasing to be writers. I understand them. I understand their exclusivity. But I must also point out that the exclusivity stems from a misunderstanding. I admit I enjoy hearing a writer railing at his mother tongue with the fury of a prodigal son; I enjoy watching a culture question its language and the established forms of the culture's relationship to its language

---

levels and can easily lead to general judgments of that nation's character. Our judgments are sometimes influenced by prejudices from other areas—politics, for instance—and sometimes national prejudices may cause us to do a disservice, unconscious as it may be, to the phonetic qualities of a language."—Miloš Weingart, "Etude du langage parle suivi du point de vue musical," *Travaux du Cercle linguistique de Prague*, 1–2 (1929), 181–82.

* A paraphrase of Anatole France: "The French language is a woman. And that woman is so beautiful, so proud, so modest, so bold, so touching, so voluptuous, so chaste, so noble, so intimate, so mad, so wise that one loves her with all one's soul and is never tempted to be unfaithful to her."—*Propos* (Paris, 1921).

develop. It appeals to me if only as a revolt against conventions and commonplaces (language being the greatest of "commonplaces"), as opposition to the generally accepted, automated forms of thinking, living, and writing. I believe that every work of value is an act of revolt against the writer's own and only language, that revolts like that of Laza Kostić* or Stanislav Vinaver or Raymond Queneau ("We are writing in a dead language") constitute an act of creation more precious than any "defense of the French language."

Which is why I wish to state here and now to those who would fear for my soul that I have no need for them to absolve me of my sin, which is to write in the language I write in, no need for their firmans or ukazes, because I do not recognize them, no need for their bulls or indulgences, because it is my language! And if we fail to understand one another in "each and every detail" ("What do people mean by their country? The place where people around them grasp each and every detail of what they say, grasp what pleases and pains them from the slightest internal or external linguistic flicker."—Isidora Sekulić†), it is not because the authors of the firmans and ukazes do not understand what I say and write; no, our misunderstandings are of an entirely different nature: they take place on the intellectual and moral level, and I refuse to allow them to impose their standards—be they linguistic or literary or moral—on me. We simply do not speak the same language. Thanks be to the Lord God of Sabaoth!

---

* Laza Kostić (1841–1910), the greatest Serb romantic poet.
† Isidora Sekulić (1879–1958), major Serb essayist and short-story writer.

Judaism

When anyone brings up the subject of Judaism or Jewishness and the sufferings of the Jews, etc., in connection
with one of my books, it gives me a queasy feeling that
cannot be fully explained as a Jewish complex or as Freud-
ian *Heimlichkeit*. As for my attitude toward Judaism and
Jewishness in general, I had adopted Koestler's cruel theory of assimilation in my thinking as well as my mode of
life even before becoming acquainted with it, though
practice, especially literary practice, rather turned me
against it. To write about Jews, to make Jews the heroes
of my writings seemed to imply a certain racial, religious,
national partisanship, and some critics, if they could have
done so, would have classified me among Jewish writers
and made me write in Hebrew or at least in Yiddish.

There was no point in trying to argue or explain, for
at the crucial moment, the moment when the nationalist
trumpets ring out (not the trumpets of Jericho!), when
you're called upon to pledge allegiance to a nation, a

province, a region, you've got to make it clear whose side
you are on, ours or theirs, because you've got to be on
somebody's side. And if they ask you again, and you say
that you side neither with us nor with them, they take it
to mean what they had secretly been thinking all along,
that you are a third something, perhaps not with them
and perhaps not against them, but in any case someone
who can't be relied on for the great union of writers and
pharisees.

If you tell them that the language in which you dream
and write situates you in our literature (though the concept might be broadened to include the literature of Central Europe or even world literature, not only in the
Goethean sense but also in the sense associated with
Borges and Koestler, as conceived and understood by
Étiemble), if you tell them that seen in that light (the light
of tradition) you are a Yugoslav writer they consider that
a kind of lie, or rootlessness, which arouses pity or anger;
they assume that by choice you wanted to hide, to mask
your true allegiance, as though you had tried from the
start, as in a race, to occupy a place in space and time, as
though you had visited all the regions of our country, all
at once, though from their point of view you are a man
from nowhere, a Wandering Jew who, thanks to your
commitment, your clear and clearly expressed literary
choices, will easily worm your way into all European and
extra-European publishing houses with wiles that are only
too well known.

In my case, however, and not only in my case, Jewishness is, psychologically and metaphysically speaking, the
unalterable sentiment which Heine called a "family misfortune" (*Familienunglück*), and I would gladly give those

of my books that constitute a "family cycle" the overall title "Family Misfortune." This sense of family misfortune is a kind of angst which, on both the literary and the psychological level, nourishes a sense of relativity and the irony that follows from it. That's all. "My Jewishness is without words, like Mendelssohn's songs" (Borges).

In addition, Jewishness—perhaps more in the case of my characters, E.S. (Eduard Scham) and Boris Davidovich Novsky, than in my own—has something of that strong, mysterious force of attraction of which Freud speaks, something of that "troubling strangeness" (which is only a free and more accurate translation of *Heimlichkeit*), and on the literary plane as well a form of defamiliarization. Seen from this angle, certain characteristics of Jewishness as perceived by Freud are not without importance for the formation of the world view of B. D. Novsky or E.S. Jewishness thus becomes a kind of latent revolt. "As a Jew," said Freud, "I was prepared to join the opposition and forgo any consensus with a closely knit majority . . ."

As for *A Tomb for Boris Davidovich* (I am thinking of the book), it contains as much Jewishness as the Bolshevik movement itself (and it is not my intention now to examine the reasons for the Jewish participation in the Communist movement) and hence as the group responsible for the "ten days that shook the world." This relationship can be expressed numerically, and I believe that an estimation based on my book would not give an appreciably different picture from that offered by the historical and archival sources: of the 246 men and women who made the October Revolution, 119 were "foreigners and Jews," of which 16.6 percent were Jews. It would be interesting to compare these figures with the data concerning the ethnic origins of the characters in *A Tomb for Boris Davidovich*.

The Jewish element in *A Tomb for Boris Davidovich* has a twofold (literary) significance: on the one hand, thanks to my previous books, it broadens and creates a meaningful tie between the mythologems I employ (and thus, through the problems of Jewishness, authorizes me to deal with the theme, insofar as authorization is needed); on the other hand, as in my previous books, Jewishness serves only as a mark of defamiliarization. Anyone who fails to understand that knows nothing of the mechanics of literary transposition.

Borges

There is no doubt: the short story or, rather, the art of the short story must be divided into pre-Borges and post-Borges. I am not thinking so much of the way he broadened the scope of reality (in the direction of the fantastic) as of the way he told his stories. The story of the Maupassant–Chekhov–O. Henry variety, which emphasized detail and created its mythologemic field by means of induction, underwent a magic, revolutionary transformation in Borges: Borges introduced deduction, which is merely another name for a kind of narrative symbolism, the consequences of which in both theory and practice are of the same magnitude as the appearance of symbolism in poetry with Baudelaire. The inductive method, after reaching its apogee in the three masters of the realistic story mentioned above, had exhausted its possibilities and—given the principle of the alternation of sensibilities and the literary reaction it provokes—feels anachronistic today.

Since such an assertion may seem sacrilegious in Yugoslavia, where we are extremely sensitive to the issue of literary realism, I feel I must invoke Shklovsky (and thus avoid the impression that I consider the new forms ideologically determined or wish to disavow "good old Chekhov"): "A work of art is perceived against a background of and by association with other works of art. The form of a work of art is determined by its relationship with other pre-existing forms . . . All works of art, and not only parodies, are created either as a parallel or an antithesis to some model. *The new form makes its appearance not in order to express a new content, but rather, to replace an old form that has already outlived its artistic usefulness.*"*

Accepting this idea, this formulation of literary evolution (which I consider basic to my own conception of poetics), does not imply any pseudo-scientific magic or dangerous (for the uninitiated) pseudo-intellectual, speculative methods by which works of art come into being; it is an approach to the theory and practice of literary phenomena that is inherent in the concept of literary sensibility, and grasping it requires no more than a passing knowledge of the history of literature and ideas. No background in theory is called for, just a bit of talent.

What is talent anyway but the ability to move away from the canon, what Broder Christiansen terms the "differential feeling" or "feeling of difference." If our critics applied this basic principle to their assessment of literature, they would have a reliable compass to work with, more reliable than their mechanical "older versus younger gen-

---

* Victor Shklovsky, *Theory of Prose*, trans. Benjamin Sher (Dalkey Archive Press, 1990), 20.

eration," "form versus content," or "the real versus the fantastic" dichotomies. And if they used the compass on my works, they would soon discover a permanent desire for "differential feeling," stop searching for the difference (with respect to our literary canon) in Jewish motifs or a special atmosphere, and turn to the constant, obsessive desire on my part to use form as a means for claiming the privilege of differential feeling; they would stop searching for Western influence (as if no other Yugoslav writer were susceptible to it) and turn to the permanent shift (in both form and content) vis-à-vis our run-of-the-mill literary production, to the distance that may not guarantee a work absolute or even relative superiority (which is a matter of talent) but does at least guarantee it modernity, that is, save it from anachronism.

If I have applied my experience with the modern European and American novel to my own works—by way of affinity, of course—it is not because by the grace of God I have managed to read works of literature or literary theory inaccessible to other mortals but because I have the feeling, the intuition that things change in the world of literary phenomena, that they shift with Hegel's famous *Weltgeist*, world spirit, and because I want to use my own themes and devices, my own mythologems, to do away with canons and anachronisms in at least the literature of my own country. Far be it from me to expect or even hope that a critic will examine my modest oeuvre* from the vantage point I have been discussing, that is, study the differential coefficient of my five or six books—from the

---

* "I accept the word 'oeuvre,' when applied to me, only in quotation marks, as a metaphor, say, but not otherwise" (Borges).

brief novel *The Attic* to *A Tomb for Boris Davidovich*—at the time they appeared with respect to the canonized works in Yugoslav literature of the period, and I have no interest whatever in their paying the proper attention to the notorious Western influence in my work (by which I do not mean the political implications the theoreticians and "wildcat critics"—as Mirko Kovač* calls them—feel obliged to see everywhere). And while Yugoslav writers seem to be the only exception to the universal rule formulated by the French literary historian Ferdinand Brunetière—to wit, that of all influences operating in the history of literature the most important is that of work on work—I would not be able to claim to be an exception to the rule, to have read nothing but Njegoš† and our folk poetry and listened only to my grandmother's tales.

I do not, therefore, reject influence; I merely wonder whether I have taken the sum of influences and used them in such a way as to create the much-vaunted differential feeling. Take the influence of the *nouveau roman*, for example. I wonder to what extent—in, say, *Hourglass*—I managed to create a genuine work of my own and turn the theory of the *nouveau roman* into a genuine novelistic world bearing a polemical and parodical relationship to its model. In my humble opinion I succeeded in doing so t least as far as the *nouveau roman* is concerned) and in proving on the model.

A Tomb for Boris Davidovich* I take up certain devices

Kovač (b. 1938), Yugoslav novelist and short-story writer.

trović Njegoš (1813–51), Prince–Bishop of Montenegro and author of *Vreath*, a long philosophical poem considered one of the masterworks introduced primarily by Borges, devices that amount to nothing more than the masterful use and doctoring of documentary material, a technique already present, though in slightly different form, in Isaac Babel (and even earlier in Poe, from whom Borges borrowed it, perfecting it in the process, as is often the case with borrowed literary devices). But while Borges tended to exploit the "documentary approach" on the metaphysical level, where the individual is perceived essentially as a philosopheme in Kafka's sense of the term, the individual in a world that is a labyrinth of metaphysical meanings (a sort of substitute for Kafka's castle) among which, as in medieval poetry and painting, the search for Soul and Essence proceeds outside the realm of history, I based *A Tomb for Boris Davidovich* on historical events, and the documents in it are meant to lay bare its historicity, man's soul having long since been given up to the Devil. Applying Koestler's dichotomy: the Borges story deals with the yogi, *A Tomb for Boris Davidovich* with the commissars.

Yet there is another type of Borges story, a type for which "Emma Zunz" and "The Intruder" might serve as models. Moving away from the metaphysical and shifting the accent from the soul to the body, they are closer to the stories in *A Tomb for Boris Davidovich*. What is more important is that in these stories, few as they are, Borges did not use documents, thus reverting in a way to the classical tradition. Even here, however, history plays no role. "Any book that fails to contain its counterbook," he writes somewhere, "must be considered incomplete." In this sense and in this sense only—as a kind of encomium to Borges—*A Tomb for Boris Davidovich* is a counterbook to the books of Borges. Not a parody, no, a *counterbook*.

"Besides, I do not know if it is necessary to say that the idea that a literature must define itself in terms of its national traits is a relatively new concept; also new and arbitrary is the idea that writers must seek themes from their own countries. Without going any further, I think Racine would not even have understood a person who denied him his right to the title of poet of France because he cultivated Greek and Roman themes. I think Shakespeare would have been amazed if people had tried to limit him to English themes, and if they had told him that, as an Englishman, he had no right to compose *Hamlet*, whose theme is Scandinavian, or *Macbeth*, whose theme is Scottish. The Argentine cult of local color is a recent European cult which the nationalists ought to reject as foreign." (Borges)*

---

*Jorge Luis Borges, "The Argentine Writer and Tradition," *Labyrinths, Selected Stories & Other Writings* (New York: New Directions, 1962), 174–75.

Individuality

The differences between the documentary approach in *Hourglass* and in *A Tomb for Boris Davidovich* are fewer than it might seem at first. In both cases this approach serves to limit the free field of invention, of the imagination, in other words, of the arbitrary. The fundamental document in *Hourglass* in this connection is the letter: it is the epicenter of an eruption but an eruption whose danger zone can be foreseen. Moreover, the concentric circles of the associative field do not go on ad infinitum as when a stone is tossed into the water; they are limited to the semantic (etymological and synonymic) field of the letter. The circles surrounding the epicenter of the explosion have less power, less destructive force the farther out they move, but the damage the splinters of reality may potentially cause is measurable by a pair of compasses (as on a military map). A stray fragment that has flown off according to the laws of centripetal force and struck shrapnel-like the roof of a house in a courtyard far removed from the field of action is nothing but a chance bit of excess, an isolated exception that confirms the rule. In such cases the "document" usually reappears, if only as a horoscope, whose sole purpose, again, is to avoid the arbitrary on the spiritual level. Not just any constellation, therefore, but Cancer, *karakata*, the sign of E.S., and Pisces, the sign of D.K.

The documentary approach is, to be brief, an anti-romantic, anti-poetic principle, a frame and a vessel, a Noah's Ark that keeps close track of the inventory.

There are many mysterious links between E.S. in *Hourglass* (and to some extent Eduard Scham in the novel *Garden, Ashes*) and the characters in *A Tomb for Boris Davidovich* (especially Boris Davidovich Novsky himself), but, more important, both works deal with strong individuals plunged into the current of history at decisive moments, individuals dragged along by the current of history yet desirous of maintaining the seal of their individuality, of "swimming against the current" in spite of it all, of cutting themselves off from the infinite mass of conformists in an era inimical to the individual; in other words, both works deal with people whose only compass is doubt—if doubt can be a compass.

B. D. Novsky and E.S. are involved in the same personal revolt, but the former is a commissar, the latter a yogi. In the end the two poles cancel each other, the yogi turning commissar, the commissar yogi. Yet their phases are distinct and separate and they are never in dialectic unity—whence the misunderstandings. They have other differences as well. The fate of E.S. is determined by historical processes and trials (in both meanings of the word), but he reacts to historical events as a yogi, that is, he centers his revolt on the metaphysical level, while

B. D. Novsky is first and foremost a social being and *Homo politicus* and therefore solves metaphysical problems in the manner of a commissar. This opposition is enough to isolate them as individuals (on the existential as well as the fictional level) and brand them, preordain them as victims. B. D. Novsky and E.S. have no desire to live and die like dogs or ants; they want to be wolves. (See, in this connection, Petöfi's twin poems "The Dog Poem" and "The Wolf Poem.")

B. D. Novsky is dragged along by the current of events, yet is at the same time their lever (as a commissar); hence the feeling of relevance and history in his revolt. E.S. is by fate and choice (existentialist philosophers are right to place an equal sign between the two) a non-participant in the creation of history, yet is determined by it; hence the shift in his revolt to the metaphysical level, to God (as a yogi), and his tragic sense of life. Rational pain, pain directed toward a goal, says Richard Rubenstein, is incomparably more bearable than irrational suffering.

THE FRENCH GARDEN

The basic characteristic of our literary criticism is its anti-individualist stance; hence the constant need to treat literature in terms of generations. The anti-individualist stance stems first and foremost from the sociological approach to literary phenomena, which holds that a work of literature is not an individual product but a collective one (like folk poetry) and that books with a certain orientation are not written by an individual but—while not "emerging from the head of the people as a whole"—are conceived at a given point in sociopolitical time and as such cannot bear the seal of an individual but only the collective and collectivist seal that is the mark of a generation.

But that is not all. The leveling influence of the collectivist, "generationist" spirit destroys the value and meaning of any book, any individual voice: one book consumes another, a good book consumes a mediocre one, a superior book an inferior one, the valuable content of one is neutralized by the stylistic imperfections of another, and vice versa, the negative points of one are offset by the positive points of another, pluses and minuses cancel one another out, and once more nothing has happened except that one generation has replaced another.

It is a no-risk situation—for the critics, at least: what they have given to one writer they take from another; they have no intention of arbitrating; they stand up for no writer, no work (except the classics, of course). Everything is equal to everything else, everything is gray or made to look gray, everything is camouflaged by a tarpaulin, everything is made to conform as in a French garden, clipped when it sticks out, minimalized, deprived of its worth—everything is "positive."

Our literary criticism is actually literary power. As such, it does not serve literature; literature serves it, the gray mass of literature production being merely the excuse for its existence. How can critics serve literature, submit to its laws, and find meaning in it when they feel that evaluating a work is a step higher on the semantic ladder than writing a work, that clearly anyone capable of judging is capable of creating and if they don't bother to do so it's only because they consider it beneath them: they have better things to do, like putting those twaddle-mongering writers in their place. What is more, critics are privy councilors, lord chancellors, who in addition to titles and the high salaries that go with them have the charge—or act as if they had it—to keep up the French garden and even lay out its paths. And if our garden looks more and more like a cemetery, we have them to thank for it.

But our critics have not only taken over the prerogatives of censorship and power; they have completely excluded the reader from the arbitration process. Moreover, they have done so not by establishing values of their own or negating, rejecting existing values, but by leveling all values, by a conscious, hardheaded process of devaluation and relativization.

THE EUROPEAN CHALK CIRCLE

Having described a "European chalk circle" (Bukovina–Poland–Ireland–Spain–France–Hungary–Russia) in space and constructed a time line of some six centuries, the objective Spirit of Narration makes a sudden appearance in the final pages as the Spirit of the Narrator, an obvious alter ego of the narrator.

A. A. DARMOLATOV

The tale of the misfortunate Darmolatov is a fable and as such the moral of the entire work.

OUR ELEPHANTIASIS

The expression "to have balls"—which apparently is not exclusively a Yugoslav or even a Slav linguistic and psychological creation—is to some extent obscurantist in nature, a praise of folly minus Erasmus, the recognition that in the world of art and (especially) literature the head merely gets in the way, the locution having rejected thought, knowledge, and spirit as superfluous or even dangerous, because everything that fails to come from the balls comes from the head or spirit, and that is bad, that is a clear sign, that is the mark of decadence, of erudition, "which inevitably subverts genuine, God-given (ballsy) talent," especially as—Skok's etymological dictionary notwithstanding—we insist on believing that the word for "balls" in our language, *muda*, derives from the word for "wise," *mudar*, whence it follows that the more balls we have the wiser we are and we should develop our balls by means of spiritual exercises at the expense of an alcohol-heavy head on its way to *Wasserkopf*dom, and the only reason our artists and (especially) writers can resist being whisked off through the air by their *Wasserkopf*s is that the gravity exerted by their balls keeps them firmly on the ground.

When we say a writer "has balls," we also mean he has a God-given talent, he is a literary stud horse, a lyrical centaur who sleeps with his God-given mistresses Calliope and Euterpe, fertilizing literature with his spermatozoa, his tadpoles—inspired by a kind of divine afflatus—wriggling and squiggling through the goo of reality to the core of things, with no compass or goal, no rhyme or reason, with nothing but his spermatozoal instinct to guide him, yet declaring all other motion in space and time with its own direction, its own logical conception of mind and spirit, to be suspect erudition, Western influence, decadent and Cartesian, depriving the individual of his testicular spontaneity. Thus, *cogito ergo sum* becomes *coito ergo sum* as motto and world view in both the literal and the meta-phorical (metaphysical) sense.

Balls notwithstanding, our centaur literature engenders nothing but the sentimental products of sentimental lovers in the outdated spirit and form of Stanković's* frenzied love stories—forty-year-olds writing epistolary novels (in prose and in verse), bemoaning former sweethearts and "vanished youth" yet incapable of generating from their dried-out scrota even our homegrown Stanković's nostalgia for youthful ecstasy, let alone Dante's heaven and hell of the soul and body or Novalis's metaphysical *frisson* or Henry Miller's (phallocratic) myth of sexuality or the tragic yet ironic erotic anguish (in the Kirkegaardian sense of the term) of a Philip Roth.

Balls are also a national stamp and racial regalia: other peoples have prosperity, tradition, erudition, history, *ratio*; we are the only ones with balls. We initiate our writers with a rigorous medieval ceremony worthy of the Vatican, the Pope, in which the lucky candidate for the title Master of Testicular Arts passes in front of all the Past Masters and each member of the Order must with his own hand satisfy himself as to the candidate's virility and testify thereto by nodding and pronouncing the magic word *habeat*, thereby acknowledging both the novice's talent and his racial and literary lineage.

Balls thus serve as a guarantee that the artist will not infringe upon the laws of the community in word, thought, or deed, and will not put his head on the block or use it in any way, shape, or manner.

---

* Borislav Stanković (1876–1927), Serb novelist and short-story writer known for his portrayal of intense passions in the context of the patriarchal order.

Schizopsychology

"Erudition is the modern form of the fantastic" is a statement made, if I am not mistaken, in connection with Borges. Brief as it may be, it contains a complete poetics of modern literature; indeed, I would call it the foundation of all modern literature. What is meant by such a formula? That the time of fabrication is past, that the reader no longer believes in fabrications, because modern times, in the constellation of the "world village" which proliferates the bizarre facts of reality, have shown Dostoevsky's famous saying, "Nothing is more fantastic than reality," to be more than a clever turn of phrase, that the fantastic quality of reality has been revealed to modern man as *fantastic reality*: the ghastly sight of a city resembling the moon's surface with two hundred thousand corpses and human bodies disfigured on a staggering scale is a sight that the medieval (*even* the medieval) imagination of a great poet could encompass only by the boldest stretch, by envisaging the sight somewhere beyond the world-here-below, in the far-off regions of eternal punishment and remorse. Hiroshima is the focal point of that fantastic world, whose contours could first be discerned at about the time of the First World War, when the horror of secret societies began to come to life in the form of mass ritual sacrifices on the altar of ideology, the golden calf, religion . . . I say "secret societies" because I am speaking of the occult: so much accumulated evil and raw fantastic reality cannot be explained by historical or psychological factors alone; it requires what McLean, together with Koestler, calls, on the basis of Homo sapiens's paranoid behavior, *schizophysiology*, the logical consequence of which is *schizopsychology*. No longer, even on the level of literature, do psychological approaches suffice, based as they are on the dichotomy of good and evil and on the moral categories man wrestles with, categories such as the Ten Commandments or the Seven Deadly Sins: allegory, that apparently most ancient of artistic (and, above all, literary) approaches to man and the world (whose chief consequence in art is what is known as psychology), has proved itself incompetent to deal with man's paranoid behavior. Bearing this in mind, the writer no longer approaches his heroes with an eye to interpreting their actions psychologically, in terms of moral consistencies or violated taboos; he tries instead, like Truman Capote and his *In Cold Blood*, to garner a mass of documents and facts which, when yoked together in a wild and unpredictable fashion, provoke a senseless massacre encompassing sociological, ethnological, parapsychological, occult, and other like motifs. To deal with such motifs in the old way would be more than senseless, for what lurks immediately behind them is man's schizopsychological behavior, a paranoid, in other words, fantastic reality; and the writer has an obligation to put that paranoid reality on paper, to examine the absurd plexus of circumstance on the basis of documents, probes, investigations, and to avoid proffering personal, arbitrary diagnoses or prescribing medicines and cures.

THE PSYCHOLOGICAL APPROACH

The psychological approach is for the most part a field of banality and the writer who works it a dilettante claiming to use his talent to expose the roots of evil (in both the social and the psychological spheres of life) and propose radical, even if no more than implicit, solutions. Cheap psychology generates cheap solutions, especially on the moral plane: the writer turns iconophile or iconoclast (either will do) in the framework of existing social plexi: church, nation, ideology, or the occult.

"MATERIAL FOR THE FORMATION OF PLOT"

Stories like the one about Boris Davidovich or any other from *A Tomb for Boris Davidovich* must submit more or less all their data to what Marguerite Yourcenar would call "the touchstone of fact." In other words, the author must renounce arbitrary fabrication (for, literary conventions notwithstanding, he is treating a historical topic and historical characters, sometimes under their own names, sometimes as a kind of identikit picture) in favor of documents and historical fact; above all, on the level of what Shklovsky calls *fabula* or "story." ("Story is in fact merely material for the formation of plot," says Shklovsky.) To invent (let us say) a man who fought on the side of the Republicans in the Spanish Civil War and was kidnapped and taken off to a Soviet camp would be, even from a present-day perspective, perfectly possible. But considering the extremely delicate nature of the topic, that is, the deeply rooted and jealously guarded conceit of a large number of intellectuals—and here I have in mind mainly those Western "leftists" who refuse to face certain clear-cut facts because they might cause deep rifts in their consciences and beliefs and require them to rethink the ideals of their youth (when everything was as pure as the sun) —considering, then, the delicate nature of the topic and the psychological blindness it has engendered, I was forced, when choosing topics for my cycle, to make use of raw material, "stories" in the Shklovskian sense, whose authenticity could not be doubted.

OBSESSIVE TOPICS

To be a professional writer here and now—that is, to regard literature as one's only passion and vocation— means to live in constant conflict with oneself and the world. With oneself because any other form of activity, no matter how related to literature, seems an injustice to one's position and talent, a compensation of sorts, a waste of time, a betrayal of one's self. Unfortunately, however, in spite of a clear predisposition to literature, I write as a "poet," not as a professional, which means I deal exclusively with my own *obsessive topics* in a kind of poetic delirium and choose only those topics and problems that obsess me intimately, that is, intellectually and morally or in a lyrical symbiosis of the intellectual and the moral. To put it more simply, I have no pre-chosen topic in mind, no bestseller-bound "theme of the hour," no order to fill; I sit down to write at that rare moment (now rarer and rarer) when my cup has overflowed, when an intellectual, moral, or lyrical dilemma or doubt has grown to such dimensions within me that I feel the need to communicate it to someone. That is what accounts for the modest size of my bibliography—five or six books; that is what accounts for the relative brevity of those books despite the obvious evidence that they have issued from a "vivid pen" or "skilled hand." It seems to me that both their brevity (typical of contemporary writers) and their fragmentary quality result from a "poetic approach" to the phenomena of reality, because it is an essentially lyrical process and cannot tolerate epic length ("inspiration is short-lived"). If there is something worthy of respect in this attitude, this sort of attitude, it is primarily that the author's skilled hand will not and cannot (for some higher moral reason) engage in literature as a profession despite all principles cogently proclaimed, despite a plain, "daily bread" mission for literature.

My first books, including the "family cycle," grew out of the youthful (yes, youthful) search for an answer to lyrical and metaphysical questions such as: Where do I come from? Who am I? Where am I going?—questions which, for various vague and fateful reasons (of race / environment / time) and despite the books themselves, are still open-ended and unclear, though no longer of burning interest to me; instead of answering them in the books, I asked myself new questions and found an ancient and apparently efficient way of releasing the lyric pressure: letting blood from the artery at the point where pressure is the greatest brought the long nightmare to an end, and I felt the release that comes after awakening from a bad dream or leaving the couch of a quack psychoanalyst. Reality (the reality of books written) has replaced the fiction of tortured questioning.

As for *A Tomb for Boris Davidovich*, it came about by a similar (unprofessional) process; that is, as the result of an obsessive topic: to have been a contemporary of two systems of oppression, two bloody historical truths, two networks of camps for the annihilation of body and soul, and to speak of only one (fascism) in my books, overlooking the other (Stalinism) with the aid of a psychological blind spot—this intellectual obsession, this moral and moralistic nightmare recently began to put such strong pressure on me that I could only resort to "letting the lyrical blood" from my artery. Having read through the abundant literature—mainly nonfiction, both leftist and rightist— on the Stalinist purges and camps, I felt shame and repentance take root and grow as a result of the obsessive thought that more or less all of us behave like Pavlov's dogs, that our conditioned reflexes are still the sole *spiritus movens* of our lyrical and epic (literary) acts, that we salivate at the toll of the death knell and the *danse macabre* of the Auschwitz orchestras, and that our conditioned reflexes of behavior and thought dictate the most dangerous of literary subterfuges, which consist in repeating stereotypes of ideas, attitudes, characters, relationships. When that thought reached its full lyrical weight, when it grew into shame and repentance, into knowledge, I started writing my stories in a sort of poetic spasm, relatively quickly and easily, like a person released from a nightmare and suffused with a feeling of well-being (despite the topic). It was the kind of spiritual relief that can perhaps be felt only by obdurate sinners after Extreme Unction.

DOGS AND BOOKS

Everything else, everything that followed, was the price I had to pay for my creative joy: all the mad whirl of literati, informers, and pharisees who have tried and still try to find meaning and justification (self-justification) in my defiant act, my coup, my attack on clichés, an area where their canine sense of smell has lost its canine acuity; who, deprived of their (Pavlovian) instincts, have stopped gobbling up the meat regularly left for them and begun instead to bark and snap, that is, to use another (temporarily dulled) set of conditioned reflexes.

The petty scrivener crowd (despite the objective attitude of the critics or because of it, despite the reading public and the [rare] well-intentioned writers) saw the book as a personal challenge, which it is, and grasped its lesson much better than I could have hoped. Then they began inventing meanings and justifications to rob it of its moral and ideological viewpoint (another area where the scriveners feel their ignorance). In their eyes—because they can think only in clichés—the book is nothing but a variation on the theme of "the sufferings of the Jews" and therefore marginal, provincial, irrelevant, questionable . . .

The dogs bark and the caravan rolls on . . .

Writing is an alchemical process, a transmutation, and the ideal metaphor and even a possible definition of the creative act involved might well be the one applied to alchemy itself: "Alchemy is the *art of transmuting* metal for the purpose of procuring gold." Needless to say, by *metal* here I mean *logos* (*logos*: word, speech, statement, feature, truth, glory, quality, order, will, reason, human concept, mind, doctrine, true doctrine, law, measure, act, proof, mathematical axiom, divine reason, germ of being, divine word, mediator, philosophical problem, law and order, necessity, legitimacy, world spirit.—*Dictionary of Philosophy*, Zagreb, 1965), logos with all its meanings as the material, the "matter," in and on which the transformation takes place, the transmutation that will lead to (if it does lead to) the "perfect metal." This creative process, taken to its extreme, does not differ in intention from that other, Eastern, variant of alchemy, in which one burns with excitement over retorts and secret formulas in the hope of obtaining a liquid, *potable gold*, which, when combined with the body's frail flesh, is reputed to lead to physical —and spiritual—immortality. The very process of writing, much like the processes of alchemy, is both mystery and mystification: everything develops in the creator's secret laboratory, that alchemist's workshop where the guild's magic formulas are not merely preserved (*salve et coagula*: purify and integrate) but enriched with personal discovery, the secret beyond secrets. For the ultimate goal is spiritual transformation, a way to reach the absolute, and that is the domain of the esoteric. "He who fails to obtain gold," says Liu Hsiang, "fails for lack of spiritual preparation."

Even when a writer parades the "secrets" of his workshop, his authorial confessions, that, too, is part of the mystification process: for they are a bogus recipe lacking a single, essential ingredient, the one he believes will turn metal or stone into gold, the one that makes him burn with excitement in his solitude. When Tolstoy disavows his art or denies it to others, he does so in a fit of para-literary integrity, of guilt over the great fraud that art per-petrates by means of art. "Literature's kitchen," he says, "repels me in a way nothing ever has before." There is a great difference between the literary theories, schools, and techniques a writer represents and his creative secrets. The best texts dealing with the secrets of creativity are accord-ingly to be found among a writer's letters, letters he did not intend to publish. Literary diaries, novels on novels, theoretical forewords, and the like—these, too, are parts of the mystification process or even (as is more often the case) simply veils to hide creative secrets.

If, then, I not only undertake such a task—the task of revealing certain "secrets" of the creative process—but use one of my own books as an example, I do so un-willingly, not because it contains any "secret" that must not be revealed to the uninitiated and not because talking about my own work like this is repellent to me in the way Tolstoy describes, but simply because, as I say, cre-ativity is mystification, a work of art is the fruit of creative ruses, and once those ruses are exposed, the work loses a part of its magic. Let me make myself a little clearer. As a child I loved to watch magicians (Shklovsky cites a sim-ilar experience): their tricks held me and the audience in the enchanted light of the supernatural, their hocus–pocus and abracadabra drove us wild, drove us into a kind of metaphysical tremor; it emanated from everything bearing the illusion of the otherworldly, the demonic, the mirac-ulous. How disenchanting at the end, when the miracle worker, a man in collusion with the forces of darkness, turned his back to the audience and showed us the reverse side of his art—the ball on the back of the hand, the knife

sliding into the sheath, the cage with the false bottom!
Why—I asked myself then—why did he do it to me?
Why did he dis-enchant me? No, I was far from happy
watching him reveal his secrets! But as soon as I got home,
I would try to do some of the ball tricks by imitating the
simple operations he showed us, and after long and ar-
duous practice sessions I realized not only that I would
never succeed but that the second part of the magician's
act, the part in which he showed us the reverse side of
his art and supposedly demystified it, was as much a bag
of tricks as the first. Not that my feeling of disenchant-
ment was any the less for it. The magic was gone, the
enchantment was gone, the belief in a certain "something," a something given only the fortunate few, communion with the demonic forces of darkness!

A work of literature cannot be shown from the other
side like a carpet, nor can it, like a translation, be com-
pared with the original. It cannot be translated into meanings other than those it contains. The reader likes to know
whether "it all happened" just as you describe it, whether
you made any changes in the actual course of events; rare
is the reader (and perhaps he is no longer even a reader
in the usual sense of the word) who knows that "it all"
does not happen, that "it all" has never happened (or at
least not as "described" in the work) anywhere but in the
work itself, be it autobiography or biography, novel or
story. The memoir is the last genre to give the *illusion* of
objectivity.

A work of literature cannot, therefore, write itself back,
reconstruct itself, any more than time or the memory of
times past (that, too, is merely a new fiction, a new reality,
a new entity, a new work). Such reconstruction is as
meaningless as the motions accompanying the reenact-

ment of a crime: the criminal brandishes a mock knife at a mock victim, playing at murder before the eyes of spectators and armed escorts. No facial spasms, no cries, no blood, no criminal, no offense, no crime.

Read through studies of literary technique; most of what you find is petty and anecdotal: how a writer writes, sitting or reclining, or standing like Hemingway (and then one day, after his death, we learn that the mystification was due not so much to "the brevity of sentence and dialogue" as to hemorrhoids!), or what writers he enjoys reading and what books—legal codes (like Stendhal), the Bible (like Faulkner), Goethe (like Mann), etc. The anecdote is nothing but an excuse for a new work, a "novel on a novel," a new mystification. Here the word *mystification* has a double meaning: on the one hand, it is the writer revealing his creative tricks and ruses or concealing new ones (from us and himself); on the other, it is the writer attempting to write a work *back*, to search for meaning in a literary work outside itself, swept away as he was by some spectacle, picture, or experience. Granted! But that, too, is mere anecdote, that is only stimulus, epiphany. The best, the only possible explanation of a work is a rereading of it!

That is why Shklovsky is right when he says that there is no point in using an author's diaries to explain the origin of a work. "Herein lurks a lie: that the writer creates and writes by himself and not *in conjunction with his genre, with the whole of literature, with all its warring trends.*"

Establishing literary kinship—that *necessary* and torturous task of the comparatist, and not only comparatist, method;

that search for the progenitor's blood type, for his tribal membership as proof of paternity and, even more, as proof of the formal features (nationality, legacy, legality of inheritance claim, etc.) of the neophyte, a foundling left at the hospital gates; the genetic method as a whole—is nothing more than a palliative, a form of mythic consciousness and reductionism (which couples genetics with phenomenology): now that we know our progenitors, no miracles are forthcoming, the mystery foundling at the gates of the world hospital has been identified by the clear-cut, *genetic* method and has received his *carte d'identité*, his civil papers, he has been given a middle initial for his patronymic, and his mother was a whore, one of the great world whores who will soon be revealed, who will soon be identified by one mark or other, by some mysterious sign as yet invisible. For, according to genetic reductionism, there is no such thing, nor can there be any such thing, as a creative miracle, there is no such thing as parthenogenesis or the immaculate conception or hidden meaning; the writer must have his progenitors, the writer may not be what he is—"all his forefathers and something more (resulting from a new 'deal of the cards' in the domain of his genetic reserves)"*—that is, creator, generator, artist, unique, irreducible, inimitable; the work may not be what it is—a miracle!

"I owe a great deal to Alfred Döblin, more than a great deal," notes Günter Grass on the jacket of the French edition of Döblin's novel *Berlin Alexanderplatz* by way of publicity, a paradoxical situation and quite intriguing: Read the

---

* Thus Alain de Benoît in reference to Koestler's thoughts on genetic (in the true sense of the word) reductionism. [D.K.]

Master (Döblin) because he influenced me, the disciple (Grass)! *"I could not imagine my prose without the futuristic components of his works, beginning with* The Three Leaps of Wang-lun *or* Wallenstein, Mountain Seas and Giants *and on to* Berlin Alexanderplatz. *Since a writer is not autonomous, since he has his sources, I can say of myself that I am a descendant of the Döblin who, before he turned to Kierkegaard, found inspiration in Charles de Coster."* As for Charles de Coster, he based *The Legend of Till Eulenspiegel* (1867) on German and Flemish sources of the Eulenspiegel legend, the previous version of which, in High German, appeared in Strasbourg in 1515 and 1519 under the title of *Von Ulenspiegel* (it has been ascribed, without cogent evidence, to Thomas Murner) and is merely a variation on the popular saga first recorded in Low German in approximately 1493 . . .

Suddenly we have set in motion a Wellsian time machine, and what do we care that in this instance it moves backwards, to time past, through the anthropological layers of the past, where we find clear traces of evidence that, far from having entered a world of pure Wellsian fantasy, we are on the trail of true scholarship, linguistic and literary.

"Panurge, a figure invented by Rabelais (and not at all identical to Cingar or Margutte), obviously represents a synthesis of figures: the average man (of the Renard type), Eulenspiegel or the *pícaro*, the wanderer, the wit, the scholar, the mystes, the *uomo universale*; he is also the forefather of various figures: Gil Blas, Figaro, Rameau's nephew, Gavroche . . . A scholar specializing exclusively in Rabelais has no chance of discovering anything new about Panurge. The only discoveries being made today come from the field of comparative mythology. Karl Kerényi, for example (in Paul Radin's book, *The Trickster*, New York, 1956), traces the image of the archetype, widely known in a number of mythologies (Indian, Greek, etc.), of the 'divine trickster,' the spirit of disorderly conduct, the enemy of boundaries, who makes possible, within the framework of a given order, what is otherwise prohibited by that order, thereby contributing to a total trickster, Hermes among the Greeks, and fathering the entire line of picaresque characters. Kerényi cites the Spanish picaresque novels, Goethe's Reineke Fuchs (though why not his medieval predecessors as well?), Thomas Mann's Felix Krull, and Rabelais. I assume he has Panurge in mind, the Panurge who plays with men and life like Hermes, god of the gratuitous."

This text by Leo Spitzer appeared in 1960 (in *Studi francesi*), the same year as Grass's *The Tin Drum*, and therefore prior to the emergence of the previously anonymous dwarf Oskar Matzerath, that composite portrait of Hermes, Panurge, Eulenspiegel, Fuchs, and Krull, the reverse side of the myth, the dwarf figure serving as a kind of defamiliarization of the titan myth of Hermes and Panurge, as an attempt at a new approach to the old theme of the mythical giant-scoundrel and doer of good deeds, a point of departure that goes against more than merely the visual and mythic grain. Once the telescope is turned back to front, once the image shrinks, all relationships change, including the relationship to the grotesque and to the ironic and parodic vis-à-vis the family of giants and the sense and tenor of the myth itself or myths of its ilk (national and later National Socialist). The moment when the telescope was turned back to front and trained on the distant past—that moment of double-edged defamiliarization, of distancing and deformation, that show of literary wit—was surely decisive, a stimulus to action: change in perspective and distance logically entails a change in literary devices, the new laws of perspective causing psychological profiles to develop in the direction of the grotesque and the polemical vis-à-vis tradition and the world. Were it not for the presence of tradition, no matter how parodic the relationship to it may be (parody merely reconfirms presence), the entire construct that is Grass's literary world would be unthinkable: it thrives simultaneously on tradition and on the negation of tradition.

The fact is that each writer has a mythical family tree of ancient and noble lineage, and his coat of arms leaves a proud mark on his manuscripts, on his palimpsest. It is like the watermark on the paper he uses, a visible sign of his origins. And when a writer begins *tabula rasa*, when his paper (symbolically speaking) lacks a watermark, he has no choice but to cite *historical* tradition and create his pseudo-family tree on the basis of a *historical* heritage, a heritage of local mythology, rather than the literary or (European) cultural heritage. Such writers are pseudo-princes and boyars with pseudo-crowns and lilies and Crosses of Lorraine, symbols galore given them to stamp on their paper as a mandate and proclaiming them keepers of the official seals and lore, of purity of language and purity of folk customs; they see their nationality as a *spiritual* dowry, as if a writer were born with a tradition, as if one's cultural heritage were sucked in with mother's milk, as if spiritual nobility did not come exclusively from the *spirit, la noblesse unique* in Baudelaire's words.

T. S. Eliot is absolutely right when he says, "[Tradition] cannot be inherited, and if you want it you must obtain it by great labour."

"Now I want to speak of a justly illustrious work which the nationalists often invoke. I refer to Güiraldes' *Don Segundo Sombra*. The nationalists tell us that *Don Segundo Sombra* is the model of a national book; but if we compare it with the works of the gauchesque tradition, the first thing we note are differences. *Don Segundo Sombra* abounds in metaphors of a kind having nothing to do with country speech but a great deal to do with the metaphors of the then current literary circles of Montmartre. As for the fable, the story, it is easy to find in it the influence of Kipling's *Kim*, whose action is set in India and which was, in turn, written under the influence of Mark Twain's *Huckleberry Finn*, the epic of the Mississippi. When I make this observation, I do not wish to lessen the value of *Don Segundo Sombra*; on the contrary, I want to emphasize the fact that, in order that we might have this book, it was necessary for Güiraldes to recall the poetic technique of the French circles of his time and the work of Kipling which he had read many years before; in other words, Kipling and Mark Twain and the metaphors of French poets were necessary for this Argentine book, for this book which, I repeat, is no less Argentine for having accepted such influences.

"I want to point out another contradiction: the nationalists pretend to venerate the capacities of the Argentine mind but want to limit the poetic exercise of that mind to a few impoverished local themes, as if we Argentines could only speak of *orillas* and *estancias* and not of the universe.

"What is our Argentine tradition? I believe we can answer this question easily and that there is no problem here. I believe our tradition is all of Western culture, and I also believe we have a right to this tradition, greater than that which the inhabitants of one or another Western nation might have . . . Anything we Argentine writers can do successfully will become part of our Argentine tradition, in the same way that the treatment of Italian themes belongs to the tradition of England through the efforts of Chaucer and Shakespeare."—Jorge Luis Borges*

What, then, does it imply to "call up" the name of another writer, of all other writers, in connection with a given writer and his work, what does it imply in the world of culture, what should it imply other than an attempt— always unsatisfactory, always vain—to probe the complex mechanism of the writer's spiritual ties and stimuli; an attempt to create an "astrological" calendar for any sign such that from place of birth, star in the ascendant, and disposition of the heavenly bodies a clear spiritual profile might emerge, the mixture of elements and ores that combine to form the writer's sensibility; an attempt to use that mechanism, the mechanical process of influences, to illuminate the mystery of his falls and, more important, the mystery of his flights, so as to draft the exact formula of the new "matter" *on the basis of its elements* and to determine the precise spiritual composition of his own, individual, unique, irreducible *Dasein*. "The mind has a

---

*Jorge Luis Borges, "The Argentine Writer and Tradition," *Labyrinths: Selected Stories & Other Writings* (New York: New Directions, 1962), 177–82.

natural tendency to give simple explanations of what is complex," says Jean Piaget, "and accept unreservedly as simple what seems so only after complexity has been diluted and processed out; and (what amounts to the same thing) the most elementary operation of the mind is one of collecting, which leads to the certitude that every complex system is the product of the common collection of simple elements. An unadulterated empiricism of this sort runs the constant risk of deforming mental reality by reducing everything to artificial 'atoms' instead of aiming at a structure of the whole." In other words, reducing the complex to the simple—that tool of provincial professors and the poor in spirit—leads to reductionism in all areas of the mind. Literature seems the chosen field for simplistic, mechanical operations: Mann equals Goethe plus the Bible, Krleža equals Matoš plus the Scandinavians (or Karl Kraus plus the Scandinavians), Borges equals Poe plus Chesterton—now we have it easy, now we have processed them into simple units like the mechanism of a clock, and if the clock refuses to start no matter how hard you shake it, well, the clock must be to blame, and it will never go beyond the provincial midnight it now points to. "Reductionism is a state of mind consisting in the certitude that complex phenomena can be grasped and explained by breaking them down into the simplest of elements; it is the naïve assumption that the simple is merely part of the complex. The reductionist believes, therefore, that he can explain everything by an understanding of elementary factors alone" (Quentin Debray). In essence, this is the sort of reductionism practiced by the critic who, knowledge and skill notwithstanding, "brings up" Borges in connection with *A Tomb for Boris*

Davidovich, especially when by a simple mental operation he reduces the book to Borges, as if it were completely and without residue contained in Borges. Never mind that all works, all important works of an age, are created under the same sign, born under the same star; they are all marked not only by the same Zeitgeist but by technical and thematic and stylistic unity (which is what makes histories of literary movements and schools possible), the same watermark beneath densely written manuscripts: each literary age has a coat of arms of its own (all nineteenth-century realist literature is *realist* regardless of the language and nationality of its author, all naturalism is *Zolaesque*, each work of expressionism *expressionist*), the same mysterious wind of mutual ties and influences blows with equal force from Japan to America. And if the concept of world literature, *Weltliteratur* (in the sense given it by, say, Borges and Étiemble), has any meaning whatever, then that is what it means. That unity. And so when the critic speaks of Borges, speaks of Borges in connection with *A Tomb for Boris Davidovich*, he, too, is kowtowing to reductionism: by establishing a common element, he reduces two different matters to an equal sign.

Establishing the presence of one or another (common) element is as far from identifying the essence of a matter —and as unreliable—as *reducing* that matter to its elements: it may be a necessary part of the operation, but it is insufficient for the crowning conclusion. The sweetness of sugar, its primary attribute, cannot be established by breaking it down into its parts: sweetness does not come from either carbon, hydrogen, or oxygen even if sugar is composed of them all ($C_{12}H_{22}O_{11}$), just as Borges (for example) is not composed of the possible (and obviously arbitrary) formula:

$$S_{30}P_{20}W_{20}C_{20}J_{10}$$

where *S* is Schopenhauer, *P* Poe, *W* Whitman, *C* Chesterton, *J* Henry James, and the subscripts indicate an arbitrary approximation of the influence of each in percentage points (and therefore total 100), even if our formula were as complicated as the structural formula of nucleic acid and even if we included *all* (or nearly all) the necessary or possible elements and combinations of elements and influences; that is, not only Schopenhauer, Poe, Whitman, Chesterton, and Henry James but also Oscar Wilde, Marcel Schwob, Shaw, De Quincey, Cervantes, Quevedo, Sir Thomas Browne, Melville, Kafka, Berkeley, Hume, Valéry, Pascal, Keats, Coleridge, Carriego, Wells, Kipling, Spinoza, José Hernández, Mark Twain, Dante, the *Thousand and One Nights*, Joyce, Gustav Meyrink, Heraclitus, Calderón, Goethe, John Stuart Mill, Zeno, Ambrose Bierce, Stevenson, Carlyle, Nietzsche, Flaubert, Parmenides, Vergil, Tennyson, Origen, the Holy Scriptures, Mallarmé, the Cabala, Swift . . . (This non–alphabetic enumeration, the onomasticon, is the system perhaps best suited to reflect the chaotic crisscross of the *prose of the world*, the magma that verbal mechanics merely *seems* to set in order, because it fails to settle into intelligible forms until after it has had its total, simultaneous impact on the person who has merged with it, who has become the whole and a part of it at the same moment. This is no place for alphabets or letters to be broken down into elements or elements to be broken down into formulas.) "The fact is," says Borges in connection with Kafka and, naturally, in connection with Borges as well, "the fact is that every writer *creates* his predecessors. His contribution alters our conception of the past every bit as much as it alters our conception of the future."

1978

ESSAYS

Homo Poeticus,
Regardless

We are exotica, we are political scandal, we are at best fond memories from the First World War and the conscience of the old *poilus d'Orient* and members of the Resistance. We are also beautiful sunsets on the Adriatic, balmy memories of beautiful, peaceful sunsets on the Adriatic, memories dripping with *šljivovica*. And that's it. We are barely a part of European culture. Politics? Fine! Sightseeing? Terrific! *Slibowitz* (as the Germans have it)? Naturally! But who in God's name would expect to find literature there? Who could be expected to make sense of their nationalist nonsense, of all those languages and dialects so close to one another yet (or so they claim) so different, of all those religions and regions?

When it comes to literature, we've got more than enough, we Europeans. Some pretty good stuff, too. While those—what-do-you-call-'em?—srbo-krkrs, well, when they deal with their sensitive issues, when they poke fun at their leaders and their system, when they write about political scandals in picturesque settings—*then* they'll have a literature of their own. We civilized Europeans, pure in heart and mind, we'll describe the beauty of our sunsets and our childhoods (like St.-John Perse), we'll write poems about love and whatnot. Why don't they stick to their politico-exotico-Communistski problems and leave the real literature—the maid of all work, the sweet servant of our childhood—to us. If they start writing about what we write about—poetry, suffering, history, mythology, the human condition, "the timeworn trinkets of plangent vanity"—we won't be interested. Then they'll be like us, with their Andrić and their Krleža (now how do you pronounce that one?) and Miloš Crnjanski (another krkr) and Dragoslav Mihajlović and so on, all of whom we can easily do without.

So *Homo politicus* is for us Yugoslavs, while they have the rest, that is, every other facet of that wonderful, multifaceted crystal, the crystal known as *Homo poeticus*, the poetic animal that suffers from love as well as mortality, from metaphysics as well as politics. Have we deserved our fate? We have. We are guilty and must bear the consequences in silence. For we have failed to resist the temptation of exporting our minor (or major—what's the difference?) problems of nationalism and chauvinism and shouting from the rooftops that we are not primarily Yugoslavs, no, we are Serbs or Croats, Slovenes or Macedonians or whatever, listen carefully, it's very important, ladies and gentlemen, you mustn't get us mixed up, some of us are Catholic, others Orthodox, we've got Muslims and of course a few Jews (mustn't forget the Jews!). So here we are, poor "Yugoslovaks" back to our family squabbles. And we wanted to talk about literature, quote

that Croat *monstre sacré* Miroslav Krleža (krkr!) and that
Serb or Croat (take your pick) *monstre sacré* Ivo Andrić,
but no, we are so clumsy we've gone and smashed the
bibelot aboli, the timeworn trinket known as literature.
Which is why we don't deserve to be taken seriously.

However—and this really is not our fault, God is to
blame—where in heaven's name are we to place this language or languages and literature? Granted it's a Slavic
language, a Slavic literature, yes, a *slavyanskaya zemlya*, a
Slavic country, correct, but with a socialist regime slightly
different from the rest. Which makes us "something like
the Russians." All right, then: all-but-Russians. At least
Russians don't make trouble. True, they come in a number of shapes and sizes (Azerbaijanis, Bashkirs, Kalmucks),
but we can always lump them together if we use the term
Soviet. So what? So nothing. No need to get excited.
There have always been great traditions, great literatures,
and small languages, small nations, just as there have always been large and small banknotes (*dixit* Andrić). So
let's be modest, keep our voices down, and try not to
drag the whole world into our family altercations.

And most important, let's not be taken in by the timeworn myth that we Yugoslovaks and other Hungarians should give up literature and stick to entertaining
the whole world with politico-exotico-Communistski
themes, give up trying to be anything but *Homines politici*,
everywhere and always, and get it through our heads that
poetry, play and playfulness, metaphysical obsessions (who
am I? where do I come from? where am I going?), and
the transports of love are not for the likes of us, that sunsets are none of our business and belong exclusively to
tourists enamored of literature and poetry and hence en-

titled to admire them wholeheartedly and with a clear conscience.

No, literature and poetry (and like Pasternak I put an equal sign between the two) are equally for us and you, our barbaric dreams and yours, our myths and yours, our loves and yours, our memories and yours, our day-to-day existence and yours, our unhappy childhood and yours (which may just have been unhappy, too), our obsession with death and yours (identical, I hope).

I am well aware that poetry (= literature) is—and is becoming more and more—the description and impassioned condemnation of social injustice (much as it was in Dickens's day), the description and condemnation of labor camps, punitive psychiatric clinics, and every variety of oppression aimed at reducing human beings to a single dimension, the dimension of a *zoon politikon*, a political animal. Yet, by so doing, it robs them of their wealth, metaphysical thought, and poetic sensibility; it destroys their non-animal substance, their neocortex, and turns them into militant beasts, naked, blind *engagés enragés*, raving ideologues. The triumph of *engagement*, of commitment—to which, we must admit, we adhere only too often and which stipulates that literature which is not committed is not literature—shows to what extent politics has penetrated the very pores of our beings, flooded life like a swamp, made man unidimensional and poor in spirit, to what extent poetry has been defeated, to what extent it has become the privilege of the rich and "decadent" who can afford the luxury of literature, while the rest of us . . .

It is a danger that threatens us all. Yet we must realize that literature—poetry—is a defense against barbarism and that even if it may not "ennoble our sentiments" it does do some good: it does give some meaning to the vanity of existence.

If only on the strength of this anthropological fact, then, we belong to the family of European nations, and have as much right as they or more—given our Judeo-Christian, Byzantine, *and* Ottoman tradition—to membership in the European cultural community.

Then, and only then, come the technical issues of translation, commentary, references, parallels, and such. The rest . . . is literature.

1980

Why Veličković's
Runners *Have No Heads*

I sincerely believe that the best criticism is the criticism that is entertaining and poetic; not a cold analytical type of criticism, which, claiming to explain everything, is devoid of hatred and love, and deliberately rids itself of any trace of feeling, but, since a fine painting is nature reflected by an artist, the best critical study, I repeat, will be the one that is that painting reflected by an intelligent and sensitive mind. Thus the best accounts of a picture may well be a sonnet or an elegy.

—*Baudelaire*

I began to think about Veličković's *Runners* when an article by a so-called art critic aroused my antagonism. The gist of the article was that Veličković painted his *Runners* without heads because he wished to depict modern man in the era of machinery and high speed, because he wished to represent the headlessness or heedlessness of the modern world. According to this critic, the *Runners* merely symbolizes the general mindlessness of the present industrial and post-industrial period, in which the individual, like a puppet in the hands of an all-powerful puppeteer, is engaged in a mad race, without definition or clear itinerary, from an indeterminate present to an even more indeterminate future, etc., etc. In certain circles this sort of "sociological" comment is regarded as the last word in art criticism.

As I see it, however, it is the worst possible way of approaching a work of art, which it takes as a mere pretext, as a useful device, while the problem of artistic expression, that complex system of relationships between form and content, boils down to a newspaper editorial and the particularity of artistic vision and execution is reduced to a meaningless generalization without bearing on *the work that is being written about.* This sort of "phenomenological" and "sociological" (or sociologistic) interpretation either demolishes or misses the point of any work it examines, for such convenient formulas as "the man of our time," "the man of the industrial era," tell us nothing about the work of art itself, and such formulas, such empty, banal thinking (which hides under the cloak of "phenomenology" or "sociology"), can be applied equally well to any work, regardless of its artistic, formal value. With its platitudes about "the contemporary world," this sort of criticism has no eye for the work which, regardless of what it may be, ceases to be anything more than a remote, inadequate pretext. These platitudes about the "age of speed" (as the futurists called it) and about the headlessness of modern man, who rushes about without aim or compass (the futurists still had their damned compass), could have been expressed in any other context (traffic accidents, for example) and would have sounded a lot better and more relevant. Precisely because this brand of criticism takes no account of the aesthetic phenomenon and its implications, it lends itself to all kinds of abuse. In "phenomenological criticism," a literary "runner with legs of lead" becomes a symbol of human anxiety and of "existential flight," etc., in defiance of all logic, even though the "existential runner" has neither the psychological nor the physical aptitudes nor the artistic motivation for cross-country racing. All "phenomenological analysis" to the contrary, an old man afflicted with cancer cannot be a runner and still less an existential champion, if only because the side effects of that ailment are anemia and exhaustion.

Thus, to call Veličković's *Runners* a symbol, an image, a representation (reflection!) of modern man, on the sole ground that his panting runners "have no heads," is to be guilty of a random association, an arbitrary statement, based on a linguistic metaphor that has become a cliché in our language: "He rushes about as if he had lost his head." But the runners in Veličković's painting have no painterly starting point (landscape in the background) or precise aim, that is, painterly perspective (landscape or background), but only arrows pointing in indeterminate directions and scales of uncertain value none of which justifies us in reducing his painterly construction, his whole painterly adventure, to "the tragic destiny of man," not even if the painter has told us in one of his statements that it was just that: "Contemporary man, who had lost his head." (But Veličković doesn't go in for theorizing; he draws, he paints. And if he accepts the suggestion of the phenomenological or sociological interpreters, I believe he does so only to avoid a confrontation, while shaking his head at the senseless formula that rejects the problem of artistic expression and reduces his formal investigations to the following message: "People without heads are people who have lost their heads.")

Veličković, however, does not paint "the headless man of the industrial era"; what concerns him is the difficult problem of form. His panting runners are simply studies of movement. Nor are they anatomical studies, studies of muscles, but just this: studies of movements and impulsions, studies of phases, "snapshots." The study of muscles is a static principle, the study of movements a dynamic principle, an attempt to capture by painterly means the movements of bodies, legs and arms, the distance between the fingers, to evaluate the maximum inclination of the big toe at takeoff, that barely perceptible movement which helps to give the body greater acceleration, however slight. The parted fingers are seeking—Veličković is seeking—the best possible means (the ideal position) of overcoming the resistance of the air; that is why these fingers were in doubt whether to cling together or open out and cut through the density, the "walls" of the air, which at this moment, when the body is in full flight, suddenly becomes dense, more dense than its own specific weight, while the body, too, becomes heavier. The body now should have the form of a bird. And that is why the fingers seek the best position in every fraction of a second, from the moment when the hand is behind the body to the moment when it is beside the body, increasing its resistance, up to the moment when the hand is in advance of the body, will clutch at the air (as we say of a man gasping for breath), and finally realize that the air, dense as it is, resistant as it is to the body's bulk, that the wind, the sirocco blowing in his face, cannot be clutched in the hand. That is why the fingers try now to join, now to part, to become webbed feet, to be used as efficiently as possible, since God has given them, just as He gave them to the duck in the form of wings (the density of the water permitting this favor). Thus, but in the opposite direction from that taken by the evolution of the swamp birds with their floating claws, the runners' hands, in this Veličkovićean flight, would traverse millions of years of evolution from one second to the next, transform themselves, evolve, equip their fingers with the fine membranes of ducks, since fingers cannot be wings. Hence the micrometamorphosis of the fingers in the drawings; hence the fingers sometimes part, sometimes come together, sometimes are motionless—their most frequent gesture being a quick perplexity, as though they didn't know what was best for them, for the body, for the impulsion, for the takeoff, for the jump. This same thought of the body and its limbs, of the feet and the hands, this same intense thought, this hesitation, can be sensed in every phase of Veličković's *Runners*, in every tendon—this same attempted correction can be sensed in every movement, every thought-reflex. And this same quest for the ideal position dictates the tangle of lines, the simultaneity of "imprecise" and never definitive movements, fixed in the precision and simultaneity of the lines. There we have the examination and the makeup examination for the runner and for the drawing, for every tendon at every moment, for the entire human machinery. (From the Renaissance to the present, from Leonardo to our own day, man, faced with the imperfect human machine, looks with envy on that anatomical miracle, the bird. Painters have one solution for this envy, for this divine injustice; technology has another.)

That is what Veličković's *Runners* are doing, that is where they are hurrying to "without their heads," where they are coming from: from Icarus to Leonardo, from one dream of flying to another. That is why there is no background, that is why there is no landscape but only arrows pointing to some indeterminate spot in the direction of the impulsion. For these runners / jumpers are pure abstraction and not a symbol or transposition of "the man of the industrial era," "the headless man of today." No, they have not lost their heads! Veličković's runner / jumper has no need of a head, the head is implied, it merely coordinates what the body thinks, what the muscles think, what the bones think, what the joints think, what the toes and fingers think, what the wrists and the ankles think, what the knees and elbows think, what the terrifying shoulders think, what the genital organs think, dangling uselessly as though measuring the precious seconds or, like an anatomical plumbline, measuring angles and verticals. In the manner of a primitive but effective instrument, these genital organs bear witness to the existence of the force of gravitation and measure its force, and on this delicate instrument the spinal column and the spinal marrow (which now, logically, perform the function of the brain as in a decapitated frog that goes on wriggling in a last reflex of the planned and programmed jump) always read the same formula: 981 cm/sec^2. Like an agitated instrument, the perturbed genital needle goes on swinging now to the left, now to the right, all the way to the end of the dial, but only so long as the machine is in flight, for at the relevant moment this sensitive needle will show that the machine has not actually moved, that the force of gravitation has been constant during the entire time of flight, that the instrument has not broken down, that its atypical behavior has been caused entirely by certain external factors or an internal magnetic storm, and that it has merely prevented the human machine from rising a few millimeters higher, the body from rising a millimeter more in space, a hundredth of a second faster.

That is why Veličković's runners / jumpers have no heads. At present they need no heads, because the head is an obstacle to the graphic execution of such a flight. And because in preparation for his *Runners / Jumpers* Veličković made documentary snapshots and film sequences (as we know, the miracle of legs in full flight fixed by camera and film has played a revolutionary role in modern art), he knows that the head is in the background, that it is neither a muscle nor a tendon but an expression, a mug, a grimace, the mimetism of the eyes, the micro-world of the facial muscles—but that is another subject. (This head is the subject of an earlier Veličković cycle, the *Loud Mouth* cycle, in which, quite logically, the body ceased to exist or was reduced to a marionette.) Accordingly, this head with its micro-spasms, its narrowed or widened eyes, its frog's mouth, belongs to another painterly world. For these runners / jumpers, however, the head is a great obstacle, the greatest hindrance (from the formal point of view): the head speaks of character, bears witness to tension, effort, decision. But here the head does not have its own movement, the head has no articulations, no joints, the ears do not move, nor does the nose—the head is static, the head is a compact, ball-shaped or egg-shaped mass, which does not move, which the body carries and supports, which merely follows blindly and passively the perfect mechanism of the body and the limbs. The head is psychology, the head is physiognomy, it is type and character, which do not concern us here; the head is sociology and phenomenology, but here it plays no role. (One doesn't look the runner or the jumper in the face, one does not see them in close-up; they are filmed in long shot and are remembered by their "style" of running or jumping.) The head, as we have said, is mere ballast. Here Veličković is not interested in studying the micro-grimaces of the eyes and the reduced technique of the mouth, grimace and effort, but only the complex movement of the limbs, their phases, their inherent dialectic. Here the head, from a formal point of view, has nothing to do. It could only introduce confusion into the perfect play and harmony of movements, it could only psychologize, philosophize, hesitate, measure every movement, accompany it with a tightening of the facial muscles, a clenching of the jaw, a creasing of the forehead, and "a glance at a distant goal" or, in the best of cases (from the painter's point of view), swing from left to right as in an attack of delirium. But that would be a psychological study of the head, a character portrait; that would be a thinking head, that would bring doubt into the impetus; the impetus would be stopped. Veličković's jumpers would be unable to jump so much as a meter if they had heads. Veličković's runners would be unable to run so much as a step if they began to think. (Look at the head of the *Discus Thrower*. It doesn't accompany the impetus of the body and the movement of the arm. The discus thrower daydreams with his head bent over his chest. Of all ancient sculptures, it would have lost less than any other classical sculpture by coming down to us without a head.) Veličković's runners / jumpers needed heads only at the start, only at the moment before taking off, while the body was concentrating to preserve its body heat, which would suddenly, at a given moment, break loose from the muscles, like steam released by a valve or a flash of intellectual decision. They needed a head only so long as they were standing on the starting line, as their gaze was measuring the height and distance of the abstraction, as long as the head was performing the quick estimations and calculations of a computer. But the moment the starting pistol rings out, the head, that useless ballast, breaks off as though it were made of clay.

Now the head is gone, the computer is gone, the calculations have been transferred to the muscular machine, imprinted on the scaffolding of a skeleton, on the network of capillaries, on the nervous system; every muscle and every movement has been programmed as perfectly as a human organism can be. Since Veličković's runners are short-distance runners, sprinters, there can be no question of tactics. Much as his jumpers long to soar, their Icarian thought ceases to be once the body plunges headlong into the empty sky, the abyss. Now there is nothing more than this midpoint between heaven and earth. They will recover their heads at the finish, if they haven't lost them on the way.

1982

Censorship/
Self-Censorship

At the height of events in Poland, just when the trade union Solidarity was being outlawed, I received a letter stamped *"Nie cenzurowano."* What exactly did these words mean? They were probably supposed to indicate that, in the country from which the letter came, there was no censorship. But they could also have meant that letters not bearing the stamp were censored, a mark of choosiness in official circles willing to demonstrate a faith in certain citizens they deny to others. They could naturally also have meant that all letters bearing this stamp actually did have to be passed by the censor.

At any rate, this symbolic and ambiguous stamp offers a profound insight into the nature of censorship. The censor wants both to establish his legitimacy and, by denying it, to camouflage his very existence. For while the censor considers censorship a historical necessity, an institution dedicated to public order and the ruling political party, he does not like to admit that it is there. He considers it a passing evil, one required by a system that is constantly embattled. Censorship, then, is only a transitory measure that will be scrapped as soon as all those people who write, whether letters or books, come of age and prove themselves politically mature, thus freeing the state and its representatives from their role as guardians of the citizenry.

Since censorship is obviously necessary—whence its transitory nature—the censor considers it abolished, *already a thing of the past*. That is why its existence goes unacknowledged by its practitioners, who seek to cloak it in the mantle of democratic institutions that serve other functions as well—the editorial board of a publishing house or a newspaper—or in the person of the editor of a book or periodical, or the director of a publisher's imprint, or a reviewer, professional proofreader, and so on. If a subversive message still gets by all these substitute censors—who perform their task in good conscience because they are not censors, not *just* censors—there remains a last resort. The printers, the most highly conscious segment of the working class, will simply refuse to print the text. This apparently democratic measure is one of the most cynical ways of hiding censorship—short of proscription of the book or article by the judiciary (a substitute for the censor) in the name of public opinion, though in fact there is no public opinion.

Among the other, less well-known forms censorship takes is the widespread phenomenon of "friendly censorship"—representing a sort of transition between censorship and self-censorship—when the editor (himself a man of letters) suggests that you eliminate such and such a paragraph or stanza from your book for your own good. If he is unable to convince you of his good faith, he will use moral blackmail and confide his fears to your safekeeping—his fate, too, depends on your willingness to censor yourself, to conceal the censorship from the public. If you don't censor yourself, you will ruin his career and his life. If you do, he will not only publish your book, he will even conceal the fact that it once contained passages that, had they been published, would have destroyed you both.

However you look at it, censorship is the manifestation of a pathological condition, the symptom of a chronic illness, self-censorship, that develops in conjunction with it. Invisible but there, far from the public eye and buried deep in the most secret parts of the spirit, it is far more efficient than censorship. While both depend on the same means—threats, fear, blackmail—self-censorship masks, or at any rate does not reveal the exercise of, constraint. The fight against censorship is open and dangerous and thus heroic, while the battle against self-censorship is anonymous, lonely, and unwitnessed—a source of humiliation and shame for the collaborator.

Self-censorship means reading your own text through someone else's eyes, a situation that makes you your own judge. You become stricter and more suspicious than anyone else could, because you, the author, know what no censor could ever discover—your most secret, unspoken thoughts, which you feel can still be read between the lines. You attribute to this imaginary censor faculties that you yourself do not possess, and to the text a significance it does not have. You pursue your thoughts to absurd lengths, to the dizzy end where everything is subversive, where even proximity is dangerous and damning.

The self-appointed censor is the writer's double, a double who leans over his shoulder and interferes with the text *in statu nascendi*, keeping him from making an ideological misstep. It is impossible to win out against this censor-double; he is like God, he knows all and sees all, because he comes out of your own brain, your own fears, your own nightmares. This battle with your double, this intellectual and moral concentration, necessarily leaves visible scars on the text, unless the struggle ends in the one and only morally acceptable gesture—you destroy the manuscript and give up on the project. But even this renunciation, this victory, has the same effect—a sense of failure and shame. For whatever you do, your double always wins. If you've got rid of him, he mocks your fears; if you've listened to him, he taunts you for your cowardice.

In the final analysis, the writer's double succeeds in undermining and tainting even the most moral individual, one whom outside censorship had not succeeded in breaking. In refusing to admit to self-censorship, the author yields to lies and spiritual corruption.

If the writer does manage to avoid radical self-destruction and, by dint of all his talent, concentration, courage, and ingenuity, does succeed in fooling his tempter-double, traces of this battle will appear in his writing—in the guise of metaphor. This constitutes a double victory: not only has the text, in spite of everything, finally got written; the ruse of reducing the idea to a metaphor (of transposing the real into the figurative) means the self-censor has transformed his idea into a figure of speech and deflected it into the field of poetics. One could draw far-reaching conclusions here, in literary history and literary theory; and on the basis of the predominance of metaphor, one could analyze the genesis of numerous literary works, for example Russian avant-garde literature of the 1920s. Self-censorship gave this literature a specific coloring and tone. Boris Pilnyak and Isaac Babel in their prose, Osip Mandelstam and Marina Tsvetaeva in their poetry, drew excellent literary effects from the fight against self-censorship. A bitter and tragic victory.

Self-censorship is the negative pole of creative energy; it is distracting and irritating; sometimes, when it comes in contact with the positive pole, it produces a spark. When that happens, the writer, overcoming his fear, kills his double, and in the violent collapse of years of prudence, shame, and humiliation the metaphors disintegrate, the circumlocutions crumble, and there remains only the raw language of action—the pamphlet. There is no more censor-double to discover what lies between the lines; everything is written black on white, down to the last atom of your discontent. (It was at such a time that Mandelstam wrote his poem about Stalin, the second one, which liberated him from self-censorship and humiliation and cost him his life.)

The moral principle kills either the writer or the literary work when it triumphs.

The censored "I," which has long suffered the oppression of fear, seizes on the pamphlet as an avenging sword. And this triumph over the censor-double has made more than one émigré writer sterile. Victims of self-censorship for years, they suddenly cross the line that separates art from propaganda and reach a phase Czeslaw Milosz has referred to as "narrowing."

What conclusion can one draw from all this? That the

act of self-censorship inevitably leads to artistic and human catastrophe, no less lethal than that caused by censorship itself; that self-censorship is a dangerous manipulation of the mind, with grave consequences for literature and the human spirit.

1985

Variations on
Central European
Themes

1

With no clear boundaries—and no center or several—
"Central Europe" is coming more and more to resemble
the Dragon of Alca in Book II of Anatole France's *Penguin
Island*, the beast with which people used to compare the
symbolist movement: no one who claimed to have seen
it could say what it looked like.

2

To speak of Central Europe today as a homogeneous geopolitical or cultural phenomenon is a risky business. Even
if we accept Jacques Morin's claim that Europe is a concept without borders, hard facts force us to exclude from
his "concept" all countries (except for Austria) that once
formed an organic part of the continent under the name
of Mitteleuropa. As for Bruno Bauer's thesis (cited by
Morin) that Europe is a community of destinies, a *Schick-*

salsgemeinschaft, I fear that after Yalta and Helsinki its only reality is in the perfect or pluperfect.

3

Even taking a historical perspective, we have trouble speaking of "Central European culture" as a coherent supranational entity, the differences in national cultures being greater than the similarities, the antagonisms more alive than the agreements. All positive cultural contacts among them date from the Middle Ages or the Renaissance and tend to be liturgical in origin: parallels between the early-fourteenth-century Hungarian and Czech *planctus*; identical verse legends—translated from Latin—in feudal Croat, Hungarian, and Czech literature; parallel Serb and Hungarian translations of chivalric romances. Somewhat later we find didactic poems common to Slovene, Croat, and Hungarian; pastoral dramas spreading from Italy via Ragusa (Dubrovnik) to lands in the north and northwest; correspondences in church legends among Hungarians, Serbs, Czechs, Croats, Poles, and Romanians even as they developed distinctive, national saints; parallels and mutual influences in the folk epic, where a common feudal ideology would over time be recast as national myth; and, with 1848 and romanticism, Pan-Slav fervor with a concomitant anti-Austrian and anti-Hungarian feeling among Slavs and an anti-Austrian and anti-Slav feeling fanned by a Hungarianized Slav, Sándor Petöfi, among Hungarians.

4

Though no "prison of nations," the universally detested Dual Monarchy, facetiously dubbed Kakania by the Austrian novelist Robert Musil, was a kind of "unwilling absolutism." If even in its heyday Musil (together with such fellow novelists as Hermann Broch, Joseph Roth, and Miroslav Krleža and the satirist Karl Kraus) looked upon the *kaiserlich-königlich* (that is, imperial-royal) monarchy as a living phantom, how much more of an oversimplification is it to view so broad and heterogeneous a region with so many national cultures and languages as a unit in our day? (By ignoring differences and stressing similarities, the proponents of this view give the mirror image of the nationalists, who ignore the similarities and stress the differences.)

5

Whether we favor a centripetal model or a centrifugal one (in other words, whether we see Vienna as the fountainhead and epicenter of culture for the entire region or Central European culture—and literature, of course—as an autonomous and self-sufficient phenomenon in spite of and in opposition to Vienna, a counterreaction to all trends originating in Vienna), the fact remains that neither has much relevance today and discussing them makes sense only in terms of literary history. A new geopolitical division of Europe has separated Vienna from her former colonies—the annexations and "natural allies" that once ringed her—making today's Budapest, Prague, Warsaw, and Bucharest closer to Moscow than to her.

6

Only after setting aside the geopolitical pipe dreams, the special interests and alliances, the local antagonisms, conflicts, and wars, the complex historical backdrop woven of mutual attraction and repulsion, do we begin to see Central European culture in a modern perspective—as a kind of "nostalgia for Europe."

7

A Hungarian comparativist, György Mihály Vajda, interprets the Hungarian nostalgia for Europe as a quest for legitimacy within the framework of a "virtual Europe," a desire "to be accepted by Europe or to adopt our own, virtual Europe, even if Europe has always stubbornly refused to accept the very existence of our language, culture, and literature." To a greater or lesser extent his words apply to every nation and language of the enclave known as Central Europe.

8

Denying the existence of a Central European nexus (as the Croat Krleža does) implies a search for one's own legitimacy and identity within the framework of a "virtual" Europe, where the concept of Mitteleuropa is untainted by provincialism, the Asian steppes, or even Viennese Secession. When Krleža states, "If Rilke had written in French, literary historians might have placed him somewhere between Samain and Jammes," he is stressing the primacy of the culturological impulse, and although he claims that literature cannot "be isolated as an idealistic constant free of social and geopolitical grounding," he allots purely literary phenomena pride of place in literature's magnetic field: "In the dying days of the typically French symbolist movement Rilke was closer to Supervielle than to any Austrian poet." By the same token, the Hungarian poet Endre Ady, though by his own account a member of the École de Paris, maintained (again, according to Krleža) closer links with Hungarian sixteenth-century poetry and Hungarian popular verse—the *kuruc dalok*, songs of the insurrectionist armies at the turn of the seventeenth century—than with anything "Central European."

9

Thus, it is impossible to ignore the unique features the small peoples and languages of the Central European enclave contribute to this virtual Europe, not only in Ady and Krleža (both of whom depend heavily on folk verse) but also in our current Serb and Croat literary cultures. "With its 'haiduk decasyllable,' which undeniably constitutes one of the underlying motifs of our literary tradition or mentality, our own romantic movement has nothing whatever in common with the Central European pattern . . . The Baroque symbiosis of our literature with that of the Italian *Seicento*, its patriarchal transmission through the gusle player, was romantic long before Mérimée's *La Guzla*, and to force it all into the concept of Mitteleuropa is a sleight of hand currently favored by certain Western-style aesthetes out of sheer ignorance of the facts" (Krleža). The Hungarian comparatist mentioned earlier lays claim to a similar literary autonomy: "Hungarian poetry did not follow Europe; it formed part of the general European literary tradition."

10

It would be interesting to learn whether Bartók used the expression Eastern Europe because he wanted to refer to the part of the European continent where East and West are merely geographical coordinates of one and the same entity or whether on the basis of the long-banked fires of its song, its *melos*—Hungarian in particular (whose archaic form is pentatonic and Asian in origin)—he regarded it as a distinct and autonomous entity, more of a piece with the Slav and Eastern folk legacy of the Danubian tribes than with Western Europe.

11

The work of the Hungarian poet György Petri rejects all connection with what we might call the Central European tradition, the cultural and literary network promoted from the turn of the century until the eve of World War II by Budapest's "Europeanizing" journal *Nyugat* (*The West*). Petri programmatically undermines, warps the carefully honed phrases characteristic of *Nyugat* writers like Dezsö Kosztolányi or György Juhász and breaks down the *fioriture* typical of Central European Secession painters into Pollock-like splashes. His anti-formal poetics stems from a radical rift with the whole Danubian (Vienna-cum-Budapest) tradition of poetry as the manifestation of the beautiful: poetry is as ugly as reality. There is no point then in "singing" it, only in growling, raving, barking, and vomiting it; there is no "refuge in solitude," no "garden of earthly delights," no platonic love or infatuation. The much afflicted Attila József comes closer to such a reality in his poetry than the brilliant Kosztolányi and his melancholy creation Esti Kornél. Traditional poetry with its nationalist, Petöfi-like fervor rings false today; it is an idealistic projection with no future, the optimistic ravings of a somnambulist. Petöfi was trampled by Cossack hooves, Ady done in by French sympathies and the

French disease, and both revolutions (1848 and 1919) ended up bloody defeats leading back, all things considered, to what they could only lead back to: the perpetual Hungarian status quo. Thus, Hungary tilts even farther toward the eastern shore of the Pannonian Sea, and "proletarian internationalism" has put an end to Petöfi's nationalist and Jacobin ideals. As for Ady's Danubian ardor ("The Danube and the Olt are one in voice"), it provokes only snickers today. The Hungarian ethnic minority in Romania (with a population of a million and a half to two million) cannot hear that single voice of rushing rivers: they are cut off from their homeland and subjected to forced Romanianization as part of a "community of brotherly peoples." Ady's birthplace lies over the border, off-limits to potential pilgrims among Hungarian poets and schoolchildren. Yet Petri's poetry is not a poetry of protest: it makes no claims, bears no message, wreaks no revenge; what it wants to be—and what it is—is a snapshot of the wasteland that is Hungary.

12

From today's perspective (and a good number of books have tackled the subject of late) it is no generalization to speak of a Viennese cultural sphere whose activities—psychoanalysis, Secession, expressionism, etc.—extended from the turn of the century until about the time of the Anschluss. An "explosion of genius," yet in an age of only relative and ultimately illusory stability, of luxury and license, an age that never quite dispelled the sense of a world in decline, of impending doom. Furthermore, we can only accept Musil's contention that what passed for Austrian culture was in fact inextricable from Vienna:

"Austrian culture was a false view of things from a Viennese perspective." Thus, Austria-Hungary was a "rich cabinet of curiosities that doubtless prompted many a useful flight of fancy yet—let us not forget—had not the slightest coherence." As for values, we must return to pre-1867 Austria, when remnants of enlightened despotism still made themselves felt. "The fact that since 1867 no one in a population of more than fifty million has expressed the same confident, enthusiastic rapture over modern Austro-Hungarian culture shows up the whole myth of our culture for what it is," Musil concludes. "Empty romanticism."

13

In a state based on no clear concept, "on neither the creative will of a single nation nor the free association of nations that might have given it a skeleton and quickened its blood" (Musil), in the "vacuum of values" (Broch) created by the anonymous, bicephalous, imperial-royal administrative organs, it was perhaps only natural that anti-Semitism should form and grow tumorlike.

14

With the extermination of the Jews throughout the Central European basin and the anti-Semitic policies of the Stalinist era (when an atavistic Russian anti-Semitism took on the sheen of an ideological struggle with "cosmopolitanism," thus awakening old demons among the "fraternal nations," especially Poland, and arming irrational instinct with the weaponry of a no less irrational ideology), with the disappearance—from Vienna, Budapest, and Warsaw—of the vein of Judaism that had given the

Central European landscape more than a tone and color, that had served as a driving force (nationalist organizations and the democratic internationalist reflexes to them took shape in connection with or reaction to the region's Jewish population), in other words, with the disappearance of Jewry as gadfly, Vienna has sunk into intellectual provincialism. By an irony of history, Vienna has become a transit point for Jewish refugees from the Soviet Union and its satellites, a stopping place on the journey to Israel and America.

15
The sudden interest in "Central Europe" is the result less of concern over a culture remaining in the shadows than of the West's growing awareness that the Manichaean East–West split has caused an entire geographical region to vanish into the mists. No sooner had Western intellectuals recovered from the dazzle of "red suns shining over our little Europe" (Morin) than they found to their amazement that the region of Europe "situated geographically in the center, culturally in the West and politically in the East" (Kundera), was gone forever.

16
Waking from a long ideological hibernation, the European West discovered that part of its own cultural heritage was missing and that it was much the poorer for it; it began to notice that a zone of Europe which the larger nations had smugly considered barbaric (minus Vienna, of course) had a literature and culture it had completely ignored. After casting a retrospective glance at this European twilight zone—which was not, after all, Asia—the

intellectuals of Europe concluded that despite the illusion it gave of being an ideological monolith its literature could not be subsumed under the rubric of Russian or Soviet literature, its supposedly rightful model. But by the time they came to their conclusion, it was too late: "Central Europe" as a cultural and historical phenomenon had become a thing of the past.

17

Perhaps all that "Central Europe" still means in terms of culture is the desire for a place in the European family tree, whose eastern branches stem from the same roots and feed on the same sap of religion(s) and of the Middle Ages, the Renaissance, the Baroque—a legitimate desire to see a common heritage acknowledged in spite of or, rather, because of differences. Indeed, the differences are what make it unique and give it an identity of its own within the European whole.

18

At present the notion of a Central European sphere of culture may well be felt more strongly in the West than in the countries that ought logically to constitute it. Their aversion to the Mitteleuropa premise derives primarily from an increasing tendency to withdraw behind national boundaries, but also from the political and (especially) ideological divisions within the region. How, given the current rigid ideological constrictions, can democratic, "capitalist" Austria, atavistic enemy of the Danubian peoples and erstwhile ally of Nazi Germany, join the Central European sphere? How can Vienna join when the literature of the left, from Karl Kraus to Miroslav Krleža, has repeatedly portrayed her as a center of annexationist and other reactionary tendencies and Austria-Hungary as the "prison of nations," reviled by Hungarians no less than by others? (Clearly this rejection of Vienna is fueled in part by the current fantastic notion—completely out of touch with reality—of a "Danubian state" based on the "legitimate right of the Habsburgs" and uniting large areas of the Danube region in a new geopolitical configuration.)

19

When casting a retrospective glance over the Central European cultural sphere as a whole, then, we must not forget the existence of national cultures and literatures, which base their autonomy not only on reciprocal differences and reciprocal repulsions (see Krleža's *Hungarica* in this regard, a blanket denial of the Hungarian cultural sphere) but also and primarily on a rejection of Vienna and the Viennese cultural sphere. The influence of French culture, incidentally, has always stood for progressiveness and opposition to Vienna.

20

From Matoš through Krleža and Tin Ujević the anti-Vienna stance of early-twentieth-century Croat intellectuals grew to encompass everything that came from the capital. They saw Vienna as the center of political reaction (which it was) and a backwater. Hence the pilgrimages they made to Paris, hence the blind eye they turned to Viennese cultural and artistic life, hence Krleža's rejection of the Secession movement. Indeed, Krleža regarded Freud, Kafka, and Rilke as provincial, hardly worth mentioning, fit only for ridicule. Of the entire Viennese nexus he seems to have accepted only Karl Kraus (for his revolutionary fervor) and Otto Weininger (for his radical nihilism) as cultural phenomena of the first order.

21

Serb culture has maintained close ties with Russia and the Orthodox Church throughout its history and harbors the mystical Russian bond to this day. Serb nationalism feeds on Slav and Russian mythology even as it rejects Bolshevism: Orthodoxy and the Russian literary tradition, Pan-Slavism and Dostoevsky, and Pushkin's graybeard Pimen from *Boris Godunov* (in the Mussorgsky version) have as much appeal today as Blok's "Scythians," Esenin, or Mayakovsky. Add to this the generations of intellectuals educated in Moscow, where they picked up European culture and socialist ideals together, and the spell of Russia is easy to understand. Just as St. Petersburg was a "window on the world" for Russians in the time of Peter the Great (but also Russia's bulwark against "decadent" Catholic Europe), so Russia is Serb culture's "window on the world," one where two myths converge: Pan-Slavism (Orthodoxy) and revolution, Dostoevsky and the Comintern.

22

Nationalism does not necessarily terminate the European connection. On the contrary. A desire for European culture often takes the form of national pride ("We are Europe") and antagonism ("And you aren't"), which is ultimately no more than a form of resistance to uniformity and Bolshevization. Thus, "bad eternity" turns into metaphysical shudder: "We are not dying alone," says a contemporary Slovene writer, "because the mildly Baroque area stretching all the way from Trieste to the Baltic, loosely called Central Europe, is dying with us. Croats, Czechs, Slovaks, Hungarians, and Poles are dying with us. I might even add Bavarians. Yes, all nations and peoples indelibly marked by Central European culture. We are not dying alone; we are dying with the Jews of the region, Central Europeans par excellence and hence the first to fall, long since transformed into crematorium smoke" (Marjan Rozanc). "All peoples have reasons present, past, or future to think of themselves as unique," says Valéry, and immediately adds, "which after all they are."

23

The work of Peter Handke, an Austrian writer of Slovene origin, owes more to Faulkner and Parisian experiments in prose than to any writer on the cultural horizon of Central Europe, past or present, while all fiction in the Soviet satellites has passed through the purges and purgatory of Socialist Realism, is generally marked by populism (a last-gasp emanation of that same Socialist Realism, though populism actually goes back to pre-1914 and interwar theory and practice in both Hungary and other countries ruled by the Dual Monarchy), and is groaning under the burden of proscription, censorship, and self-censorship, of party directives and the impossibility of communicating with "the world," that is, Europe or even Vienna, which is now "on the other side" and thus seems an ocean away from the onetime Central European cultural centers of Budapest, Prague, and Warsaw.

24

The ultimate goal of the ideological struggle waged for the past forty years in the "lands of real socialism" against "decadence" in art and all branches of culture is homogenization and Bolshevization. The epithet "pro-Western" is thus an ominous political attribute meaning anti-Soviet, anti-Communist. If certain secondary aspects of "Western culture" (like experimental poetry or pop music) are tolerated nowadays, it is more a consequence of "revolutionary tactics" than a prelude to something more.

25

In the fifties you could be expelled from school in Yugoslavia for wearing tight trousers of the sort probably worn in the West and as such considered hooliganism and a dangerous political deviation. At the time I found it a complete mystery: how could narrow ties and narrow trousers pose a threat to the system? Then one day I saw a Soviet delegation that had made the trip from Dubrovnik to Cetinje (where the National Museum presented it with a rifle that had been captured in one war or other and had belonged to the royal family). Baggy trousers flapped about the dignitaries' legs, and their ties had the huge knots I picture in Moscow's Bohemian cafés on the eve of the Revolution.

26

When the wife of a Hungarian writer, the product of a successful cross-fertilization, was asked by Kosztolányi's widow, "Where are you from, my beautiful child?" (in a kind of Central European version of Snow White), she replied, "The Carpathians," a response no less ambiguous than the query. Later, in private, the beautiful woman's lucky husband recounted to me his theory of assimilation, which, though identical to Koestler's, he had clearly arrived at on his own. "I am fifty percent Jewish by blood. My wife is the same. In two generations, even that will be lost. Being Jewish is a curse." Here, too, he was unconsciously paraphrasing someone else, this time Heine: "Being Jewish is a *Familienunglück.*" A family calamity.

27

Besides the frustration of classical anti-Semitism, Central European Jewish intellectuals have experienced two major traumas: fascism and Communism. And while the fall of fascism (assuming they came out of it alive) might have lent them, as it did West European Jewry, the ambivalent status of victim, the coming of Stalinism, largely championed by Jews, denied them the fruits of liberation. Add to this the uncompromisingly anti-Israeli line of the countries under Russian domination—a policy dictated as much by Realpolitik as by anti-Semitism—and you will see why throughout the Central European basin talking or writing about being Jewish is a source of embarrassment and guilt for Jews and non-Jews alike.

28

Kafka—writing to his father—on Judaism: "I did not see what else to do with so heavy a burden than to rid myself of it as soon as possible. The very process of doing so seemed to me an act of the greatest piety." Despite the clear strength of conviction in this passage, Kafka did not stay long on the path of renunciation. A Jew, says Sartre, is someone others take as a Jew. His life is one long flight from others and himself.

29

Psychoanalysis, that quintessentially Viennese phenomenon, is still regarded in Russia and her satellites as a "decadent" and "cosmopolitan" ploy to make an ominous crack in the monolith of Bolshevik ideology for which no approach to human phenomena and actions beyond the "scientific"—economic and social—model can exist. As ideology is the sole *spiritus movens* of behavior, obscure subconscious or irrational forces have no place in the scheme of things.

30

If we can speak of the existence of a Central European intellectual without unduly fearing the Hegelian fusion of identity and non-identity, it is primarily Arthur Koestler's doing. Hungarian–Czech–Jewish origins provide a kind of horoscope to the quests and contradictions of Koestler's life: from Judaism to assimilation theory, from Marxism to the utter repudiation of Communism, from a flirtation with Eastern spiritualism to its demystification, from a faith in science to the mistrust of all "closed systems of thought," from a search for the absolute to serene resignation vis-à-vis man's critical faculties. Koestler's intellectual adventure, all the way to his "ultimate choice," is unique even on the broad European spectrum, yet it incorporates the potential biography of every Central European intellectual: it is its most radical realization.

31

There is no explaining the Karl Popper phenomenon—
the radical relationship to the European philosophical heritage, the epistemology, the vision of an open society—
outside the context of Central European culture. What
makes Popper different from other philosophers and de-
termines his negative attitude toward totalitarianism and
its advocates is nothing if not the Central European *dif-
ferentia specifica*.

32

Why is it when I read the works of Andrzej Kuśniewicz,
a Pole born in 1904, or Péter Esterházy, a Hungarian born
in 1950, I find something in the way they put things that
draws them close to me, a Central European poetics if
you will? What is the tone, the vibration that situates a
work within that magnetic field? Above all, the inherent
presence of culture: the form of allusion, reminiscence, or
reference to the whole European heritage, a consciousness
of the work that does not destroy its spontaneity, a careful
balance between ironic pathos and lyrical flight. Not
much. Everything.

33

Since even the awareness of belonging to a culture known
as Central European is ultimately an act of dissidence,
writers whom others call Central European or who define themselves as such generally live in exile (Milosz,
Kundera, Škvorecký) or are marginalized and appear in
samizdat (Konrád) or are in prison (Havel). Like Jews
eager to prove how integral a part of society they are,
they come to realize that their nonconformity stems from

a certain reserve and an almost unconscious yearning for broader, more democratic, European horizons—the precise charges leveled against them. If they are not yet in exile, they will end up there. Or in jail.

34

Once exiled from the home of their language, writers are left with nothing but that language; it is the mark of their exile. They go on writing in it as if the high price they have paid made them the only ones able to resist the "exile of syntax." And if they have escaped the perilous semantic homogenization of newspeak, it is primarily because they are keenly aware that as writers they use more than words alone: they write with their entire being, with ethos and mythos, with memory, tradition, and culture, with the impetus of linguistic associations—with everything that the automatism of language turns into the flick of a hand (and vice versa).

35

Language is destiny. Every attempt to tamper with a writer's linguistic integrity is hazardous, fraught with danger. Even Nabokov experienced the passage from one idiom to another as a trauma. "My private tragedy, which cannot, and indeed should not, be anybody's concern, is that I had to abandon my natural idiom, my untrammeled, rich, and infinitely docile Russian tongue for a second-rate brand of English, devoid of any of those apparatuses —the baffling mirror, the black velvet backdrop, the implied associations and traditions—which the native illusionist, frac-tails flying, can magically use to transcend the heritage in his own way." *Even* Nabokov, I say, to stress not so much his close contact with English (and French, for that matter) as the fact that he was a *Russian* writer. Because ultimately—had he been willing to make certain concessions—he could have gone on writing in Russian. Like a number of other Russian writers in exile (Bunin, Zamyatin, Solzhenitsyn, Sinyavsky), he would not have been totally deprived of a voice or an audience. (The fate of the poet is much less enviable.) Given the long, solid tradition and worldwide recognition of Russian literature, Russian writers are in a much more favorable position than their Central European counterparts. Their roots are known: they do not set off empty-handed into the world, into exile; the Russian literary tradition is their *lettre de noblesse*, the proof of their lineage. Central European writers go it alone: their family libraries are suddenly worthless; their appeal to literary ancestors falls on deaf ears.

36

Exile, which is merely a collective name for all forms of alienation, is the final act of a drama, the drama of "inauthenticity." Central European writers have long been caught between two kinds of reductionism: ideological and nationalistic. Though tempted by both, they have learned that the ideals of an "open society" lie in neither, and find their ultimate legitimacy exclusively in language and literature—the "strange, mysterious consolation" spoken of by Kafka. Dangerous yet liberating attachments: "a leap beyond the killer's ranks." Yet the commitment is not untainted by doubt: no one abandons a community without regret. Betting on eternity is as vain as betting on the present. Hence the constant sense of "inauthenticity."

37

The French critic Marthe Robert argues that Kafka's K. stands for more than his own initial; it is an indication that he is unable to lay himself bare. Not only do I feel her interpretation to be accurate; I feel it goes beyond Kafka. That lone letter, both masking and telling, can stand for any Central European writer. K. is a sign of eternal ambivalence.

38

Were I to say that awareness of form is one of the common traits of Central European writers—form as a desire to make sense of life and metaphysical ambiguities, form as the possibility of choice, form as an attempt to pinpoint an Archimedean fulcrum in the chaos surrounding us, form as a bulwark against the mayhem of barbarism and the irrational caprice of instinct—I might only be generalizing from my intellectual and literary obsessions.

1986

The Mediterranean and the Golden Fleece

Among the spectrum of issues raised by the key concepts of my talk, "Mediterraneanism and Atlanticism," there is one I feel certain we shall fail to satisfy: the issue of definition. Nor, I might add, shall we arrive at a definition of "intellectual hegemony." Where may intellectual infiltration be considered necessary or useful, and where does "hegemony" set in?

As the title of my talk implies, the identity of our Mediterranean countries is critically threatened by the intellectual hegemony of Atlanticism. Rubrics like "A Sea of Peace in the War Against Pollution" and "The Mediterranean: Cradle of Culture and Civilization" invoke cultural history, anthropology, ecology, and the like, and we must broach our topic from a number of angles—economic, political, social, cultural—so closely knit that none can be excluded. I do not claim to be saying anything new, though I do feel that as *Kulturträger*, "people of culture," we should not let ourselves be carried away by the sociocultural side of things.

My fear is that we may be led to alter our thesis and —instead of addressing Atlanticism and its hegemony— start criticizing and condemning industrial civilization. For what is Atlanticism, primarily, but the hegemony of industrial civilization, and that is a European rather than an Atlantic matter, the backlash of a long historical process. (The economic aspects of Atlanticism opposed in France by General de Gaulle—the privileged position of the dollar and American investments—are clearly still in force today.) But regardless of our political convictions we must not—as people of culture—forget the fact (and I do not say "alas!" because facts are not psychological categories) that the world is caught between two superpowers, two blocs, that our poor Mediterranean lies more or less halfway between the two at a point where the waves might theoretically meet, and that all we can do is register the harbingers of the clash.

It is a commonplace of history that the tsars of Russia dreamed of the Mediterranean as a Russian sea. Their dream is dreamed to this day. At a conference—similar to this one—on "Contemporary European Literatures and the Mediterranean Tradition" held in Zagreb in 1973, the Polish delegate entitled his talk "Poland Is a Mediterranean Country," and the Soviet delegate stated in connection with the Mediterranean tradition: "It must not be forgotten that Prometheus the Titan, enemy of the gods, was chained to a cliff in the Caucasus." The latter statement reveals the highly significant fact that the Soviet delegate could not separate the Mediterranean from personal considerations, that she viewed it as part of her history (Prometheus having been chained to the Caucasus Mountains). She also mentioned that Jason and the Argonauts "in their search for the Golden Fleece sailed to Colchis" (Colchis being the Greek name for western Georgia). This statement is clearly metaphorical: I would take the liberty of translating the Golden Fleece of the Mediterranean moving in the direction of western Georgia as technical civilization, that is, Western technology moving in the direction of Russia. I would also point out that she stresses the word *bogoborets*, "enemy of the gods, theomachist."

Because Mediterranean culture and civilization are, as we know, religious and theist, the most basic meaning of the myth resides in the opposition between the mythical, theist culture of the Mediterranean and the theomachist, atheist power personified by the Titan. Let me quote the conclusion of the Soviet delegate's short paper (which was entitled "The Tradition Controversy"): "For all the majesty of its culture the Mediterranean is not the whole world. I need not return to the dawn of time. In our own day the cultural explosion in the countries of Latin America, the more recent and no less powerful explosion in the countries of Black Africa, and the contributions of the peoples of India and Vietnam to world culture—all this compels us to broaden appreciably the concept of cultural tradition, of a common cause, of the dignity of all nations of the world, those still struggling for freedom and independence, for a life worthy of the name human, and those that have won this fundamental victory and are creating new, more perfect forms of social life." Here the concept of tradition expands to take in the whole world, while the concept of cultural tradition is reduced to the "struggle for freedom and independence." We could perhaps support the Soviet delegate's claim were there not certain points still requiring elucidation. "I am glad," she said, "that the memory of the Bogomils and Albigensians has been revived by the representatives of France, Bulgaria, and Yugoslavia, thereby incorporating the revolutionary and national-liberation traditions of the peoples of Europe into the concept of the Mediterranean tradition." Surely you will agree that the general tenor of her talk is that the Mediterranean tradition is nothing but atheism and revolution and that the very concept of Mediterranean culture is simply a variant of the concept of world culture as she sees it.

Thus the text I have cited contests the whole identity of Mediterranean culture and civilization, recommending ideological pollution in place of Coca-Cola bottles. Since my brief paper is meant merely as a warning, I will not expand upon the way in which our lyrical Mediterranean is polluted not only by the industrial waste floating on its surface but also by the ideological waste appearing in the above text as a sign of clear ideological hegemony that brooks no discussion. I merely wish to draw your attention to the danger of one-sided views, of double standards, of the little intellectual game of calling the nasty Coca-Cola bottle floating on the water a mine while ignoring the real mine below the surface.

One more thing: an important Mediterranean culture, one of the oldest, the culture of the Hebrews (from the vestiges of whose alphabet and literature the literature of Israel was born), received one of its most destructive blows not from Atlanticism or Atlantic hegemony but from the Soviet Union, which during the thirties and forties (or, to be more precise, between 1937 and 1952) liquidated *all* Hebrew and Yiddish writers and with them the rich Hebrew and Yiddish literary tradition. Yet the tradition has lived on in America, giving us first and foremost that great writer Isaac Bashevis Singer, whose works bring Jewish Poland to life again. Mediterranean Poland, as the Polish delegate said.

My words, I repeat, are no more than a warning, a reminder to turn an unbiased eye to matters of culture so that we people of culture can make the best of the modest means at our disposal to keep our good old Mediterranean, "the cradle of European civilization," from becoming little more than *reliquiae reliquiarum*, a relic of relics. And of course I am in complete agreement with you and your—our common—concern for the spiritual integrity of Mediterranean civilization and Mediterranean cultures (as difficult as they are to define) with respect to any hegemony, Atlantic or otherwise.

Let me conclude with a rather long quotation: "The West, which is no longer capable of viewing culture as anything but an appendage to politics, has never understood what happened in my country before 1968, just as it has never understood the 'massacre of Czech culture' that was the most prodigious consequence of the 1968 Russian invasion . . . For what was destroyed was not opposition culture but culture pure and simple. Everything important and authentic had to be destroyed . . . If the sixties can be seen as the gradual Westernization of a socialism imported from the East, the 1968 Russian invasion can be seen as the definitive colonization of a Western country. And everything the West has created since the Renaissance (yes, the Renaissance so despised by Solzhenitsyn)—tolerance, doubt, intellectual pluralism, the personal character of art (and man, of course)—all this was not merely temporary but part of a long, patient, consistent strategy meant to shift a country into the sphere of another civilization." That is how the exile Milan Kundera views the issue.

1980

Advice to a
Young Writer

Cultivate the suspicion of reigning ideologies and princes.

Keep away from princes.

Do not soil your language with the jargon of ideologies.

Believe you are more powerful than generals, but do not use them as a measuring rod.

Do not believe you are weaker than generals, but do not use them as a measuring rod.

Do not believe in utopian projects other than those you yourself create.

Be equally proud to prince and populace.

Do not allow privileges gained by your literary craft to trouble your conscience.

Do not confuse the curse of your choice with class oppression.

Do not be obsessed by the urgency of history or believe in the metaphor of the train of history.

Do not therefore jump aboard the "train of history": it is merely a foolish metaphor.

Never forget: once you reach your goal, you miss all else.

Do not write articles about countries you have visited as a tourist; do not write articles: you are not a journalist.

Do not believe in statistics, figures, or public statements: reality is what the naked eye cannot see.

Do not visit factories, collective farms, or construction sites: progress is what the naked eye cannot see.

Keep your distance from economics, sociology, and psychoanalysis.

Do not pursue Eastern philosophies such as Zen Buddhism, etc.: you have better things to do.

Bear in mind that imagination is the sister of falsehood and therefore dangerous.

Do not team up with anyone: the writer stands alone.

Do not believe those who say that this is the worst of all possible worlds.

Do not believe in prophets: you are a prophet.

Do not be a prophet: your power is doubt.

Let your conscience rest easy: princes do not concern you, for you are a prince.

Let your conscience rest easy: miners do not concern you, for you are a miner.

Rest assured that what you failed to say in the daily press is not lost forever: it is compost.

Do not write on command.

Do not bet on the moment: you will regret it.

Do not bet on eternity: you will regret it.

Do not be content with your lot: only fools are content.

Do not be discontent with your lot: you are one of the chosen.

Do not seek moral justification for those guilty of betrayal.

Beware of "terrifying consistency."

Beware of false analogies.

Trust those who have paid dearly for their inconsistency.

Do not trust those who make others pay dearly for their inconsistency.

Do not argue that all values are relative: there is a hierarchy of values.

Accept princes' gifts, but impassively, and do nothing to deserve them.

Believe that the language in which you write is the best of all languages, for you have no other.

Believe that the language in which you write is the worst of all languages, though you have no other.

"So then because thou art lukewarm, and neither cold nor hot, I will spew thee out of my mouth" (Revelation 3:16).

Do not be servile: the prince will take you for his gatekeeper.

Do not be arrogant: you will be taken for the prince's gatekeeper.

Do not let anyone tell you that what you write has no "socially redeeming value."

Do not imagine that what you write has "socially redeeming value."

Do not imagine that you yourself are a useful member of society.

Do not let anyone tell you that you are a social parasite.

Believe that your sonnet is worth more than the speeches of politicians and princes.

Believe that your sonnet is worth less than the speeches of politicians and princes.

Have your own opinion about everything.

Do not give your opinion about everything.

Words cost you less than anything.

Your words are priceless.

Do not speak in the name of the nation: who are you to represent anyone but yourself!

Do not side with the opposition: you are below, not against.

Do not side with power and princes: you are above them.

Combat social injustice, but do not make a program of it.

Do not let the fight against social injustice divert you from your path.

Study the thought of others, then reject it.

Invent no political program or any program: your inventions are of the magma and chaos of the universe.

Beware of those who propose final solutions.

Do not be a minority writer.

Question any organization that claims you as its own.

Do not write for the "average reader": all readers are average.

Do not write for an elite that does not exist: you are the elite.

Do not think of death or forget that you are mortal.

Do not believe that writers are immortal: that is academic twaddle.

Do not be tragically serious: that is comic.

Do not play the clown: warlords are used to being amused.

Do not play the court jester.

Do not imagine that writers are "the conscience of humanity": you have seen too many scoundrels among them.

Do not let anyone tell you that you are a nobody: you have seen that warlords fear poets.

Do not die for an idea or encourage others to die.

Do not be a coward; scorn cowards.

Bear in mind that heroism exacts a high price.

Do not write for holidays and anniversaries.

Do not write eulogies: you will regret it.

Do not write funeral orations for national heroes: you will regret it.

If you cannot say the truth, say nothing.

Beware of half-truths.

Do not take part in general rejoicing.

Grant no favors to princes or warlords.

Seek no favors from princes or warlords.

Do not be tolerant out of good manners.

Do not force the truth on people: why argue with fools?

Do not accept the idea that we are all equally right in the end or that there is no accounting for tastes.

"If two interlocutors are wrong, it does not mean they are both right" (Karl Popper).

"Admitting someone else is right does not protect us from another danger: that of believing everyone is right" (Idem).

Do not argue with the ignorant about things they have first heard from you.

Have no mission.

Beware of people with missions.

Do not believe in "scientific thought."

Do not believe in intuition.

Beware of cynicism, your own included.

Beware of ideological platitudes and quotations.

Have the courage to call Aragon's poem in praise of the GPU* an abomination.

Do not seek extenuating circumstances for it.

Do not let anyone tell you that in the Sartre–Camus controversy both men were right.

Do not believe in automatic writing or "deliberate vagueness": your goal is clarity.

Reject all literary schools imposed upon you.

Should the term Socialist Realism come up, change the subject.

When asked about "the literature of commitment," keep your lips sealed: leave it to the academics.

Should anyone liken a concentration camp to a prison, tell him where to get off.

Should anyone tell you Kolyma was different from Auschwitz, tell him to go to hell.

---

* Predecessor of the KGB, the Soviet Secret Police.

Should anyone claim that Auschwitz killed lice not people, ditto.

Should anyone claim that it was all a matter of "historic necessity," ditto.

"Segui il carro e lascia dir la gente" (Dante).

1984

On the Marquis de Sade

The titanic figure of the Marquis de Sade, "huge and terrifying" (Swinburne), complements the great French Revolution, whose contemporary he was. While the Revolution settled accounts with history, mercilessly shedding blood in the name of earthly progress, the "divine Marquis" wrestled with the heavens. Hence the difference in goals, amount of blood shed, and crimes (Sade being the more extreme, of course).

Sade was a Promethean rebel: the Revolution, for him, was only a pretext, the pale shadow of a metaphysical battleground. Hence his quarrel with it, his desire to go beyond it, his demand for radicalization: *Français, encore un effort!* His hatred of all institutions—with religion heading the list—is merely an outward sign, an illustration of his premise of a world without God: as it is not given to us to penetrate the mystery of creation or the meaning of the world, our conscious life is an intellectual outrage.

On the basis of this theodicean position Sade may be

classified among the heirs of gnosticism or, rather, of gnosticism's radical wing, which sees the world as the work of an evil spirit—the victory of demonic powers over the powers of good—and therefore professes debauchery and crime and refuses to procreate. Sade's characterization of nature as indifferent is more an expression of his gnostic pessimism than of the positivism prevalent among his Encyclopedist friends.

Sade radicalized the fundamental question of philosophy, the question of whether God exists, that is, whether the world is a meaningful concept with a purpose of some sort or a product of mere chance. The consequence of his conclusion—negative, of course—was commensurate with his monumental disillusionment: if there is no God, if human life is no more than a brief and brutish adventure and the world mere absurdity and chance, then not only is everything permitted, but crime is the nec plus ultra of human nature. In addition, crime is an act of rebellion, the only act compatible with our knowledge of the world, the only act at least partially capable of appeasing our thirst for eternity, for the unattainable meaning of existence. "If eternity of being in nature is impossible, then disillusionment is a law of nature."

Sade's gnosticism finds its prime opponent in Christianity because Christianity represents submission—acquiescence to the world order—and consolation. He much prefers paganism, the pagan deities—unlike their monotheistic counterpart, "who fills all with His immensity"—being mere semi-mysteries, symbols of vital forces, images of human passions. And even if he extends his metaphysical revolt to earthly domains—history and society, morals, institutions—it is only a minor part of a vast gnostic revolt, a "secondary heaven," the outward form of the invisible struggle going on within his soul, the soul of the "divine Marquis."

Having arrived early in life at the basic conclusion that there is no God, the Marquis de Sade decided that instead of stoically accepting the world (as his stance would seem to have warranted: how can one fight against Nothing?) he would opt for revolt. If the word *opt* has any meaning here. Because his decision was more the cry of an afflicted soul, a plaint of all too mortal flesh, than a consciously thought-out concept or philosophical doctrine (gnosticism). And what could be more logical in a world without God than to choose the flesh, the mortal human body, and the ideology of crime as the object of revolt?

For Sade crime is a philosophical category comparable to Descartes's *cogito*, a means of intervening in the affairs of nature and the only way humans can in fact revolt. For if there is no God, says the terrible Marquis, all morality is hypocrisy and every life a defeat. Hence his response to his own scholastic question "Is murder reprehensible in the eyes of nature?" is an unequivocal no. "Nature is what prompts man to murder and advises him to kill."

In a world of universal relativism, a world with no past or future, sensual pleasure is the only present. It is not a way of giving existence meaning; it is a way of fulfilling its absurdity. It is not a victory over nothingness; it is a sovereign gesture of despair, the attempt of a mortal to achieve dignity by transgressing prohibitions, to stand up against the cruelty of nature and the horror of the indifferent heavens by engaging in debauchery and crime. Given this overweening ambition, this monumental task, debauchery is Sade's hard labor, a painful and exhausting, monomaniacal and monotonous undertaking despite the monstrous imagination he uses when coupling his subjects.

They know no limits: they fornicate like the gods on Olympus and offer up human sacrifices in a kind of bloody pagan rite. Eros and Thanatos go hand in hand in Sade's world, a world of shrieks and moans where blood and sperm flow in equal measure and passion's panting and death's rattle alternate and commingle in a general copulation without joy or love or lovers' games: everything is in dead earnest, everything is drudgery, a demonstration of the gnostic doctrine that man is hurled into the world as into a sewer. If we listen more closely to the death rattles and look more closely at the convulsed, panting bodies, we shall find that we have clearly and unmistakenly left this world for Hell. Sade thus shows us his Chosen Moment in the eerie light of eternity: he experiences it *sub specie aeternitatis*. While reveling in its functions, its destructive élan, the flesh is about to decompose into the eternal prey of eternal hellfire as in Dante. But in Sade there is neither Purgatory nor Paradise, all is nothingness—*nada*, as the Spanish has it—and the bodies pairing, the bodies lashing and gashing one another, are the image of a relativism that annihilates pain and pleasure both. The Marquis's copulations are rituals as grim as they are cruel; nothing could be further from love or the joy of lovemaking. The monstrous scenes of copulation flowing from his overheated brain come closer to somber medieval mystery plays than to Rabelaisian carnivals. The boudoirs and mysterious castles where the orgies are enacted are, for all their luxury, as cold and bare as operating rooms because Sade knows nothing of the luxuries of the diurnal world; he cares no more for, say, landscape than for the riches of human personalities or psychological states. Debauchery is the predominant human state, the only one worthy of attention, and all individuals, male and female alike, are mere stereotypes of Homo sapiens with no distinctive features other than those relating to their (hypertrophied) sexuality. Even the distinction between the sexes serves primarily to point up how arbitrary it is at the decisive moment, the moment of general copulation, when sexual boundaries quickly lose importance: if everyone copulates with everyone in every possible manner, the male–female principle blurs like kinship distinctions in the face of incest. This is debauchery in its primal state, debauchery as sublimation: nakedness not as a naked body but as a naked idea, a clear thesis: Alas, there is no God.

In Sade's monstrous choreography of generalized incest, social barriers crumble as well: servant and master give themselves to each other by turns, deriving an intensified pleasure from the infringement of convention. Like the transgression of all boundaries—sodomy, incest, torture, crime—the violation of social norms serves to arouse the senses. But only for a moment, only until the master has consummated his miscegenation. Then servant can follow master no further. "Narrow is the way." There is only one plank bridging the chasm that must be crossed, and it is a plank with room for only one: the master. For the way is the way to death; that is, punishment for the miscegenation to which the servant (man- or maid-) has succumbed (just as torture—now that only the master derives pleasure from it—is reduced to punishment). And since servant cannot accompany master into Supreme Debauchery, the old hierarchy, forgotten for a time, returns. Only a man for whom fornication is a religious act, the ritual immolation of a victim (or a parody of same), a philosophical postulate, is entitled to Supreme Debauchery; he alone can lay claim to the prerogatives of the Supreme Being, he alone can dispense death. In the castle, a logos in miniature, Sade imitates the mechanisms of the universe, parodies the absolutism of nature, her cruelty and indifference. That is why his world knows no mercy, no compassion, no repentance.

If the world is beyond our reach—"for man is not fated to penetrate to the origins of things"—the only act of despair and revolt open to an enlightened gnostic is the mimesis of nature. In this sense Sade has merely radicalized Enlightenment philosophy—its materialism, its vitalism, its cautious atheism—juxtaposing the pessimistic idea of man having been hurled into the world to the idea of progress: because man aspires to the absolute, he can know no consolation.

Sade's pessimism is among the bleakest, the most basic and destructive known to philosophy. For while other fatalistic doctrines eventually preach acceptance, passivity, Nirvana, Sade's pessimism is aggressive. From disillusionment he derives rage; he has something of the rage of the conquistador. Man is a mound of flesh, blind passion, a copulating machine; all is convulsion and pain, all is sweat, blood, sperm, and the only human words—issuing not from the veins of the tortured victim but from the breast of the torturing voluptuary—are "I am dying." Nor are they a mere metaphor (metonymy) for passion at its peak: they are a surrogate for passion: to have an orgasm is to die, because the orgasm is the only biological clock that tells the exact time, every orgasm is a small death, climaxing means dying a little. As the French say, *"Partir, c'est mourir un peu."*

Despite the boundless erotic fantasies that go into them, Sade's works are abysmally monotonous: "Nothing happens." After the first copulation only the number of partners increases and the *figurea Veneris* alternate; after the first crime, the first shock, it all starts up again, turning round and round on itself—more figures, more crimes, more screams. The main weakness of erotic literature is repetition and monomania.

The Marquis de Sade once said of Voltaire: "Having no other intention than to put philosophy into his novel, he abandoned all else." The same holds for Sade: he, too, "abandoned all else." His works are nothing more than brilliant illustrations of a single obsessive idea—that human existence is a failure. "Virtue and vice shall lie in the tomb together, side by side." His inflamed imagination worked with a single material, human flesh, and his covetous eyes concentrated on a single nocturnal sky, the *nox microcosmica*, which medieval anatomical atlases situated in a circle whose center is the groin and whose circumference does not surpass navel and knees. In Sade the *nox microcosmica* grows into a vast cosmic darkness without stars and without God—into the Apocalypse.

1988

Two Variations
on Flaubert

IDIOTS AND MARTYRS

Until Flaubert, literature was a whole (recall Balzac), a totality of world and being, a pillar of life and society on the order of army, government, philosophy, state, family. With Flaubert began an age of "decadence" that has lasted to the present. Literature lost its dominance, its integrality.

Literature has had a hard time learning to live with the tragic awareness of a paradise lost. Witness Flaubert's vain attempt—through the work itself (*Bouvard and Pécuchet*, for example)—to recover its totalitarian status, its now unthinkable universality. He seemed not to realize that the world had been smashed to smithereens, that a previous static model had been forced into motion, that the age of the fixed easel was gone forever. He hoped to repair the *zerbrochener Krug*, the shattered jug, at all costs. Hence his style, hence his martyrdom. If prose did not disappear entirely after Balzac, we have mainly Flaubert to thank for it.

"Decadent" literature, born with Flaubert, has lasted, through Joyce, to the present. Aware of a unity gone forever and reconciled with the loss. Aware that it is doomed to fragmentation, yet hoping by means of fragmentation to provide a comprehensive vision of the world and humanity. In *The Temptation of St. Anthony* Flaubert used documents from the past to locate a possible fixed point in this world of inconstant structures, thereby founding a literary school Foucault calls "the Fantasia of the Library."

Flaubert thus taught us that style is an entity unto itself and ushered us into an extended family of idiots and martyrs.

1980

FLAUBERT AND BORGES

Thanks mainly to his correspondence and to the traces of creative effort clearly visible in his manuscripts, Flaubert's quest for the *mot juste*, the right word, and his *affres de style*, torments of style, are now legendary. His unique creative drive resulted from a suspicion he could never quite shake: that there was a gap between his intentions ("No one has ever imagined a more perfect type of prose than I") and his practice. Poor Flaubert believed the fault lay somewhere in him, in his talent; he did not realize that after Stendhal and Balzac a certain *form* of fiction was on its way out. The genre itself, as the formalists would say, had begun to weaken.

Flaubert appeared on the scene too early and, though within reach of a solution, was unable to make a radical break with the tradition of the realistic genre. His weakness stemmed from doubt: he sensed the arbitrary nature and the limitations of the psychological novel. Hence his flight into the exotic, where—because the reader could not hold them to the psychological standards of the age—characters had greater integrity, greater freedom of action.

Yet even in *Madame Bovary* he came to express implicit doubt as to the omniscience of the narrator and the art of psychological portraiture, those most pernicious and persistent of literary conventions. The further the plot progresses, the more his doubt intrudes. As the psychology of his protagonist eludes him, clear-cut statements ("She began to think of Les Bertaux") are hedged ever more frequently by expressions of equivocation ("Should she write to her father? It was too late, and *perhaps* she regretted not having given herself to the man," or "She had let herself be seduced by his words and even more by his voice, by his whole personality, so much so that she pretended to believe him or *perhaps* did believe the reasons for their parting").

One word, *perhaps*, was the first step on the road from psychological to modern fiction. By pointing up the abyss between the omniscient and the skeptical ("unreliable") narrator, it served as a sign that the genre was aging, a strand of gray in the luxuriant tresses of the realist classics.

Had Flaubert compressed the vast edifice of his exotic novel into a story reporting the contents of an imaginary and complex work entitled *The Temptation of St. Anthony*, had he reduced the material for *Bouvard and Pécuchet* to a story explicitly containing part of that material (which is easy to imagine, given that the Borgesian idea of "presenting false bibliographic data as genuine" had in fact occurred to Flaubert), literature would not have had to wait a century for Borges's *Ficciones*.

1986

Karlo Štajner,
Witness for the
Prosecution

DEAD SOULS

In June 1956, the highest officials of the Soviet and Yugoslav governments—Khrushchev and Tito and their
chiefs of staff—were sitting in the saloon car of a special
train speeding from Moscow to Kiev. There was no need
for an interpreter. Since the agenda was full (a number of
ideological differences that had accumulated during the
eight-year Yugoslav "schism" remained to be cleared up),
there was no time for long talks. But at one point, when
the host (Khrushchev) seemed in a good mood, Tito
reached across the table and, as though proffering a menu
to a guest, handed him a list of dead souls. It was a Gogolian scene. "Here is a list of 113 former Yugoslav officials who have never returned from the Soviet Union.
What has become of them?" Khrushchev glanced over
the list and passed it on to an aide, saying, "I'll let you
know in two days." Exactly two days later, over the
drinks and cigars that followed the official round of ne-

gotiations, Khrushchev announced, as if in passing, tap-
ping the paper with his pudgy fingers, *"Tochno sto nyetu"*
(Exactly a hundred are dead).

Orders from on high then set the monstrous machinery
of the KGB in motion to locate the thirteen remaining
Yugoslav Communists in the immense wilds of Siberia,
and somewhere among the living dead in far-off Kras-
noyarsk they found Karlo Štajner, who after some twenty
years in prisons and camps had been sentenced by the
Ministry of State Security to internal exile for life. (An
internal exile was considered a "free man.")

Štajner: "All I knew was that Tito was alive . . . That
news had reached us. When I was in exile in Malakovo
I saw a newsreel from the time Khrushchev was in Belgrade and confessed what he confessed. It had a few shots
of Yugoslavia, and I thought I recognized Djura Cvijić
sitting on a reviewing stand somewhere. I wondered what
position he held now. A member of the Politburo at least.
We'd been good friends, so I wrote him a letter (in care
of the Yugoslav Embassy in Moscow)."* Irony and tragedy came together in the Gogolian world of dead souls:
the friend of his youth and former Party official had been
dead for eighteen years when Štajner wrote him that letter; he had been liquidated in a Siberian camp or Butyrki
prison.

NO SCARS

It is 1976, and I am sitting in the bar of the Hotel Inter-
continental in Zagreb waiting for the famous exile and

* From an interview in the journal *Ideja*, 2, 1981.

author of the celebrated *Seven Thousand Days in Siberia,*
which had been an invaluable guide for me as I worked
on *A Tomb for Boris Davidovich.* In fact, I dedicated one
of the stories in the book to him.

All of a sudden a vibrant, energetic gentleman—well
built, of medium height, and with closely cropped hair
(he has his hat in his hand)—comes up to the table. That's
not him, it can't be.

"My name is Štajner."

Even allowing for the fact that twenty years had passed
since his return from Siberia—time enough for the
wounds to heal—I wonder: Where are the scars? Just as,
according to Solzhenitsyn, a murderer's face bears the
mark of his deed in the form of a vertical line at the corner
of the mouth, so the victim's face should bear some trace
of the deed. Christ has his stigmata.

"Somewhere in *A Tomb for Boris Davidovich,*" this mild
man says, free of anger, free of pathos, "your hero takes
an evening stroll around the Kremlin. You really ought
to correct that when the book comes out again. Anyone
caught prowling around the Kremlin at that hour would
be arrested before he knew it, especially a foreigner like
your character." I promise to have it corrected by the next
edition. That and several other things he suggested.

I ask him what I can order for him. Anything at all, he
says. "I'm drinking vodka," I say. Slightly embarrassed—
he doesn't mean to offend me—he says, "Oh, no, thank
you. Anything *but* vodka. I haven't touched the stuff for
twenty years and have no intention of starting now." We
settle on a French cognac (in memory of the good old
days), and he goes on.

"At one point you mention wallpaper. Really, young

man," he says, with a dismissive wave of the hand, "there was no wallpaper in Russia at the time."

I try to explain I had found a reference to wallpaper in an encyclopedia and used it because it was so bizarre, because it *seemed* an anachronism. That, too, he dismisses with a wave of the hand, like a man accustomed to being disbelieved even when what he says is obvious. (But where are the scars, I wonder, gazing into his gentle, sincere eyes. Where are the scars?)

LA FEMME EST L'AVENIR DE L'HOMME (LOUIS ARAGON)

On another occasion, again in Zagreb, Karlo introduces me to his wife, Sonya, a Russian, to whom he dedicated his book: "This book is dedicated to my wife, Sonya, who waited faithfully for me." Any comparison or association with the mythical Penelope would be an insult: while Penelope spun at her loom for twenty peaceful years under the clement skies of Greece, rejecting numerous suitors and winning the admiration of her fellow citizens, Sonya—in the updated, Soviet version of the myth—was humiliated, spat upon, tortured as the "wife of an enemy of the people." That was what happened to women who refused to repudiate their husbands publicly. "Many women had been arrested for having 'connections with an enemy of the people'—that is, with their own husbands. The punishment for this was usually ten years in a camp in the extreme northern latitudes of Russia, or banishment to Siberia. The children of arrested parents were put in special NKVD homes, unless relatives volunteered to adopt them—but that, too, could incur suspicion of having 'connections with an enemy of the people'; that

is why many people chose to conceal their family relationship to victims of the NKVD."*

Eyes Deep as Wells

How much of all that Sonya experienced in twenty years
of waiting we do not know. All we know is the part told
in Karlo Štajner's book. At the time of his arrest Sonya
was in her last month of pregnancy. The girl who was
born died of want, cold, and illness. Then came long days
of waiting, lines instead of the loom, drudgery, making
the rounds of the ministries, fearing a knock at the door,
hoping for letters that seldom came, setting aside every
kopeck so as to send a little something to Karlo . . . I
repeat: any comparison with the mythical Penelope would
be a cheap device, an insult to Sonya Štajner.

I look at her and lower my eyes. I cannot sustain the
glance. Sonya Marmeladova is pure human suffering, a
literary character in the worst sense of the term—paper,
poetry, and joie de vivre—while in the eyes of this other
Sonya, Sonya Štajner, eyes sunk deep in the face of a
beautiful woman (a woman still beautiful), I discover
something I have never seen before: dead eyes! Not like
the eyes of the blind, blind eyes; no, eyes the likes of
which no writer has ever described and few people have
seen: dead eyes in a living face. (Even now I am helpless
before those eyes, because if no one has ever described
such a phenomenon, I am talking about something the
reader cannot visualize, and psychological explanations are

* Karlo Štajner, *Seven Thousand Days in Siberia* (New York: Farrar, Straus and Giroux, 1988), 26.

useless.) Sonya Štajner's eyes are not void of expression; they are dead, like the eyes of a corpse. Their gaze is glassy, petrified; they retain only the ash of a former flame, hot ash, not whirlpools but deep wells where the light of the sun cannot penetrate, eyes deep as wells, where, bending over, you see only clear, still, dark green water, wells reflecting only spent stars in a dead sky. With a deep furrow running between them. The mark of a martyr.

Now, only now, and indirectly do I find what I had been searching for in Karlo Štajner: the twenty years, the more than seven thousand days he spent in the farthest reaches of Siberia, above the Arctic Circle. The humiliation, the beatings, the fear, the hunger, cold, and death.

A Brief Biography

Karlo Štajner's biography resembles thousands of biographies in Europe, particularly Central Europe. The pattern is familiar: the son of a proletarian family sets forth on a path of struggle and idealism ultimately leading to the "Third Rome," Moscow. Here is how Štajner sums up his early years in a typewritten note: "Born in Austria early in the century, he joined the leadership of the Communist Youth at the end of the First World War while working as a typesetter. He worked in the Communist Youth International. In the twenties he established excellent relations with Yugoslav Communists and soon came to work permanently in Yugoslavia. Following Party orders, he set up and ran a press in Zagreb to produce clandestine Party publications. He collaborated with many Yugoslav revolutionaries, carrying out a number of missions and traveling widely. He was imprisoned in Zagreb, Paris, and Vienna, employed by the Comintern in Berlin, and in 1932 sent by the Yugoslav Party to Moscow. A month after his arrival in Moscow, where he reported, as instructed, to the Balkan Section of the Comintern, he was given a highly responsible position: he was named head of the Publishing House of the Communist International. He spent nearly four years in that position and still held it when he was arrested in the autumn of 1936."

The rest is known; it constitutes the substance of *Seven Thousand Days in Siberia*.

THE FATE OF A BOOK

"In the dungeons of the NKVD, in the icy wastes of the extreme north—wherever my suffering had passed beyond the limits of endurance—I held fast to one resolution: to survive, in order someday to tell the world and especially my party comrades about my terrible experience."*

The manuscript of Štajner's book was ready in 1958, two years after his return from Siberia and the same year as Solzhenitsyn's *Gulag Archipelago*. What happened to the manuscript between then and 1972, that is, for the next fourteen years, is a story in itself, and although Štajner did not write a book about it he has revealed part of the mystery in the *Ideja* interview: "The manuscript lay there for several years. It couldn't be published. The publishers were willing, but somebody stood in their way. I submitted one copy to Zagreb, another to Belgrade. Both

---

* Ibid., xv.

disappeared. That's right, disappeared, without a trace. So I was told. But I'd kept the original in a safe place: with my brother in Lyons. Siberia had taught me a thing or two.''

Since world politics also depends on personal responsibility and the stance of the individual, however, the book was given the go-ahead in 1971, apparently with Tito's approval. It received one of the leading Yugoslav literary prizes, the "Book of the Year," awarded in honor of the Yugoslav poet and partisan martyr Ivan Goran Kovačić. Four more years passed between the first Yugoslav edition in 1972 and the first foreign edition, in Germany. And, outside of the French edition of 1981, that was the only translation of Štajner's work. I know for a fact that out of personal gratitude to Tito, whose intercession saved his life, and out of Party discipline, which he apparently respects to this day (Štajner joined the Yugoslav Communist Party in 1919 and is thus one of its oldest living members), he declined an offer by an American publisher because the man had published Milovan Djilas. Or so the Comrades led him to believe. Sonya, too, her well-deep eyes full of fear, told him, "Be careful, Karlo." And foreign publishers could not bring out the book until it had appeared in Yugoslavia. "I wanted it to come out here first," he said in the *Ideja* interview.

Once the book was out, however, mysterious things began to happen. The Yugoslav Authors' Agency, which serves as an intermediary with foreign publishers, received option requests from a number of West European and American publishers and wrote to Štajner that the Agency would be happy to talk to him about the possibilities. So Štajner went to Belgrade. "It seemed important," he said.

But there a woman who worked for the Agency told him, "I've been ordered to stay out of it and I advise you to sever all contact with foreign publishers." (Sonya: "Be careful, Karlo.") Manuscripts of the work began to get lost abroad as well. "The same thing happened with the Italians . . . I went to Florence for a meeting. They took me to a house on the outskirts of town. I said to myself, 'Christ! if I get out of here alive, it will be a second Norilsk.' They looked like a bunch of killers, sitting there smoking. Some publishers! I hadn't been so scared in years. Still, I left them the book. I wasn't surprised to learn it got 'lost.' No one knows the man whose house I went to. When I inquired at the publishing house, they said nobody by that name worked there. Well, I had no doubt as to who was involved."

Thus, Karlo Štajner's vital testimony has reached French readers some twenty years after the manuscript was completed and ten years after it was first published in Yugoslavia. But at least it has reached them.

THINK FOR YOURSELF

In 1977, Štajner was asked by a young leftist after a lecture in Belgrade, "Did you remain true to the ideas of your youth during your twenty years in the camps?"

"We prisoners were cattle," he replied without hesitation. "We were reduced to the lowest biological instincts and the most elementary existential needs. There was no place for ideology; our only ideology was survival." Many members of the audience, which included students from Austria, Germany, France, and Italy, began to stir in protest: Štajner had failed to utter the cliché invited by the question and designed to absolve minds muddled by ideology and teleology from all sense of guilt. But Karlo Štajner had more faith in his own intelligence and *biological* experience than in any ideology; he was "intellectually mature" in the moral sense Kant had in mind when he said, "What is enlightenment? Enlightenment is intellectual maturity, and its motto is: 'Have the courage to think for yourself.'"

1981

Nabokov, or Nostalgia

Until the scandalous *Lolita* and its scandalously wretched film version, Nabokov was virtually unknown outside Russian émigré circles and a narrow set of devotees. In that period of great upheavals, neither critics nor readers expected much from this magnificent *talánt* (in Russian, accent on the second syllable), while mediocre writers, floodlit against the literary sky, and their political allegories blown up into short stories or thinned out into novels, achieved enormous popularity.

At that time, Nabokov remained a solitary aristocrat (in the Baudelairean sense of the word, an aristocrat of the spirit), remote not only from world events but also from the traditional political struggles into which so many émigrés threw themselves body and soul and which rewarded them only with hangovers and the bitter taste of defeat. In both Berlin and Paris he had seen countless talents burn themselves out in the flames of political passion and nostalgia, in polemics, feuds, poverty, and madness, escape into messianism, Pan-Slavism, Occidentalism, spiritist evocations of the Russian past, Orthodoxy, nationalism, anti-Semitism, betrayal, espionage, palmistry and Nirvana, or else, driven by homesickness and equating Bolshevism with populism, return to Russia and spiritual servitude, the firing squad, or suicide.

Sirin-Nabokov* understood the vanity of these passions in time; he saw the absurdity of all the Russian émigré governments, clubs, parties, and circles flirting with fascism, Bolshevism, Trotskyism, and the NKVD (which incidentally on the eve of the war had its privileged hunting ground in the West, especially in France, where it bagged big tsarist game no less than small Trotskyist partridges). In the brilliant stories he published in Russian émigré journals, he portrays the members of this unhappy émigré society, incapable of assimilating into the local population or of even engaging in useful political activity (if only to open the eyes of the streams of French tourists to the fact that they had been shown Potemkin villages in the Soviet Union) or—in spite of their talent—in creative endeavors. Nabokov realized that there was no hope of opposing the Star of Bethlehem rising in the East, promising to fulfill all the hopes of unfortunate mankind and put an end to the blind power of history, which now at last would be guided by human will (and not by irrational forces of necessity), that the Hegelian *Weltgeist* was irresistible for the time being, and that a writer's best bet was to ignore the somnambulist attraction of the Great Illusion and "cultivate his garden."

* In 1921, Vladimir Nabokov adopted the pseudonym Vladimir Sirin for his Russian writings.

Thus he found himself isolated from all—he who by the logic of his origins should have been able to devote his pen and his mind to a "higher cause," to write about past glory, the exploits of the vanquished, about rivers of blood and grandiose crimes. He would have been hated and glorified, he would have been a messiah and a victim, a living scandal, Solzhenitsyn before Solzhenitsyn, Panait Istrati and Victor Serge rolled into one. But Sirin-Nabokov wrote about the Bolsheviks (who appear quite incidentally in these stories) without hate, with the same detachment as he wrote about people with whom he (may have) sympathized; he wrote as though observing the world from the sidelines, askance, directing the lens of his camera at the drooping stockings of a former prima donna, at the bald pink skull of a famous general, at the trembling fingers of an alcoholic poet; he magnified the hairs in the nostrils or the rotten teeth in the mouth of a countess nibbling a sandwich (a *buterbrodik*) on a local train.

Surely either in the Berlin of the twenties or in the Paris of the thirties and forties, Nabokov could have found sufficient witnesses and collected sufficient direct, oral or written, testimony of Soviet reality (earlier and more reliable than Koestler's, for example) and thus become a key witness to an epoch. Being a witness does not preclude literary mastery (see Babel, Pilnyak, etc.). For Nabokov, however, history was the illusion of an illusion. And if he overlooked the crucial fact of the twentieth century—the camps—and rejected them as material unworthy of his pen, it was not only because he did not wish to waste his life in vain polemics but also because he placed his bet on eternity rather than on the moment. (Nineteenth-century

Russian literature gave him enough examples of glorious victories and glorious defeats.)

Nabokov's conception of the world and humanity is an idealistic one: the world is mere appearance and art is a reflection of the Platonic models, the image of a lost paradise. The artist is the double of the Demiurge, and his world is only remotely connected with the outward aspects of life: "Imagination is only a form of memory." He therefore rejects all art that is based on current events: "A work of art is of no interest to society . . . What protects a work of art from moths and rust is not its social significance but solely its artistic value." Nabokov views the political animal (*zoon politikon*) with contempt because it is devoid of idealism: its world is empty and so simplified that it cannot be the object of art. And when one cannot dream, one had best keep silent.

Convinced in his way of the potency, the omnipotence, of art (and culture), he turned into a scoffing parodist when depicting the reactions of the political animal: tyrants, like vices, he felt, can be exterminated by mockery. He also believed—and he may have been right—that the world of barbarism can be combated only by the world of art, that even if art does not act directly on people and events it can, like music, slowly but surely temper human nature.

This conception of art may well have come from his "rich nostalgia"—the world surrounding him in Russia was a world of kindness, beauty, and love (which are perhaps the same thing), a world of culture, in which art, poetry, and music made deep inroads on the human heart. The fact is that Nabokov saw only the sunny side of Russia, nests of noblemen, blond princesses, urbane and cultivated individuals, whereas the seamy side, the crude and cruel world of muzjiks and misery, passed him by as though seen through the windows of a Pullman. That is why, little by little, his "timeless Russia" became a mythical country, the Zembla, a fairy-tale country without geographical identification, Vinland, Courland, Zoorland, a Terra Nabokoviana, where people speak "a Nordic tongue," an imaginary childhood language.

Nabokov's art derives its emotional charge from the first twenty years of his life, those passed in Russia; they are the source of his arsenal of images, his wealth of imagery, the wellspring of his inspiration. The Russia of his childhood is his lost paradise, his Paradise Lost, its images and archetypes (*pardon, maître!*) feeding his writing to the end of his days, with exile merely stimulating his nostalgia. Like Alice / Anya he passed through a magic looking-glass and found himself in Wonderland, a fairy-tale country that seems as familiar to him as one of Pnin's linguistic misunderstandings, for it was indeed a *Vaterland* and bore a close resemblance to Russia at the turn of the century. This enchanted realm has castles surrounded by parks, where butterflies flutter and true princesses stroll as in the novels of Tolstoy. One of the princesses is so much like a certain Mashenka / Lolita that one might be led to believe that when princesses pass through the looking-glass, they are punished by emerging as coquettes and debauchees.

Nabokov experienced the loss of the paradise of his childhood in a scholastic sense as the fall of the angel. And in this fall the work of divine machination, the role of history, is negligible.

The whole of Nabokov's work is nothing if not a segmented Proustian *recherche du paradis perdu*, and his butterflies, the ones in his books and the ones he chased throughout the world (one of which, like a distant star, bears his name), are only a symptom of his eternal nostalgia, the sole proof his paradise existed. His lepidopterian myth, which he cultivated consciously and stubbornly, is merely a response and a challenge to a "bestial century" (as Mandelstam called it), a sign and message: while the world howls with the wolves, the Master-Demiurge leaves his ivory tower, a tower of ideas closely resembling the chess piece, and chases butterflies, those flying flowers which are the presence of art in a world without God, and infinitesimal (material) proof or scholastic argument for the existence of paradise, for the *possibility* of its existence.

Hell as antithesis, the radical evil of our century—Nabokov had no desire to consider them or approach the flames more closely than is permitted to mortal man. For there reign chaos, sound and fury, its landscapes are gray and cruel like the Kolyma of the unfortunate Varlam Shalamov. Where civilization and culture have ceased to exist, where man's spiritual and moral qualities have been destroyed, there is no place for Nabokov's characters or for parody, and games or memory. Nabokov's world is too domesticated, too humanized, too policed. The "aesthetic shudder," the tingling that creeps up the spinal column, "the highest form of emotion, which humanity achieved when it discovered pure art" (V.N.) has long become anguish and trembling, the fear of death. It is their timelessness that makes Nabokov's novels seem as anachronistic as their nineteenth-century counterparts. Their themes and techniques make them slightly frivolous fairy tales. A magnificent, complex, and sterile art, to paraphrase Nabokov's characterization of the art of composing chess problems.

Nabokov wished to oppose the world of barbarism and chaos to a world of order and form, to give art back its role of Demiurge, to rehabilitate the classical model of master and mastery. Like the *"poètes maudits,"* he created an artificial paradise in which there is no opium but poetry, and he peopled this paradise with hominids—all his characters are to some extent somnambulists or dream characters moving in a world of illusion, beyond good and evil, and the terrible tumult of history barely reaches them. These creatures of dream and memory, these fallen angels, are devoid of blood, or else their blood is blue and violet like ink; they are the fruits of immaculate conception and subject to an eternal erotic longing, a medieval erotic dream; children are brought into the world without pain and people die easily—in the last chapter with a stroke of the pen—like pieces toppled on the chessboard returning to their nonexistence.

And yet Nabokov's condemnation of a certain variety of literature and of certain writers is more moralistic than aesthetic. All his work—his stories and novels, his essays, lectures, and interviews—his whole stance, is a fervent plea for the preservation of spiritual values, a polemic against spiritual chaos, against the stupidity of the age, against false values, against the brand of criticism that judges works of art by non-aesthetic, psychological, or (God forbid!) psychoanalytical criteria. If criticism has not quite degenerated into lunacy, if literature has not become the handmaiden of ideology but remained a dream and an escape, a play of the spirit and the imagination, an act of culture par excellence, we have in large part the master-magician Nabokov to thank for it.

1986

INTERVIEWS

All the Genes of
My Reading

For months now, your fourth and most recent novel, Hourglass, *has captured the attention of the critics. They have rarely been so unanimous in their praise. Is* Hourglass *meant to complete the cycle you began with* Early Sorrows *and* Garden, Ashes? *All three are linked by time, atmosphere, and characters.*

Hourglass is the third and last book of my family cycle, and only as a trilogy does the true nature of the three novels become clear. Together they depict—on separate levels and with an odd sort of parallelism—not only the general development of the two main characters, who seek and complement each other throughout, but also their coming of age in a creative sense: if you take the character by the name of Andreas Scham as a stand-in for the writer, then you can take the three novels as a sort of literary Bildungsroman.

In Hourglass *you chart the hero's consciousness and his neurotic defense mechanism of accepting the inhuman realities of war as the only possible means of survival. Does this mean you find tragedy essentially impossible?*

The hero's consciousness is only one of several layers in the novel. The other layers take a kind of objective, documentary approach (albeit fictional) as a way of reconstructing not so much the hero's mind as his world—the Zeitgeist, if you like, presumptuous and high-flown though it may sound, the *Weltgeist*, all the elements which went to make up that world—as a way of dispelling the clouds that enveloped a world now gone forever.

I avoided jumping to conclusions; I tried as far as possible to be impartial when judging people and events, to maintain as documentary a narrative tone as possible—except, of course, when E.S., the character the book is mainly about, used me as his medium. E.S.'s bias is beyond reproach: it is the bias of a man scared to death, the bias of the clairvoyant, of the madman.

Judging from the many biographical clues in the novel, Eduard Scham is your father. Tell us something about the role autobiographical data play in the novel's structure.

It is difficult, impossible even, to separate the autobiographical element from a work. The only one able to identify it is the writer, yet there comes a time when even the writer is confused—given the logic of things and the power of the imagination—about what is fact and what is invention. This happens even with memoirs, let alone fiction.

Faced with this phenomenon, I tried to justify the duality, find an alibi for it, in the opening chapters. Hence, for instance, the image of the hourglass with its two facing profiles (a symbol of the creative principle). An author implants thoughts in a character in the belief that the two consciousnesses will complement each other, that the two experiences of life will "move closer to each other, as though wishing to unite and so confirm their identity."

To put it more precisely: the existence of documents bearing on my father obliged me to be faithful to them, just as the existence of his letter (which closes the novel) kept me from speaking of things not in it—or at least not touched upon, hinted at, inherent in it.

Owing to the mosaic-like, patchwork structure of Hourglass *and its strikingly modern approach, the full meaning of its sixty-seven heterogeneous fragments does not become clear until the final pages. Was it the magnitude of the fear, violence, misery, and death you portray that made you reject the chronological structure of classical epic narrative?*

Hourglass has a very clear chronological line to it, a precise order of items and events: everything in the novel occurs in the course of a single night, from the moment E.S. sits down to write at sixteen minutes before midnight (Chapter 16) until shortly before dawn the following day, "civil (morning) twilight," that is, about four o'clock the following morning (Chapter 62); everything that occurs occurs in E.S.'s mind within this very clearly defined chronological order in the dead of night and of the soul, when laws other than those of chronology prevail—laws of association and organization.

The other element governing the novel's development is the letter and the phenomena and associations it sets in motion. It is no coincidence that two chapters are entitled "A Witness Interrogated": the letter that serves as my structural principle, my ground plan, makes two separate mentions of a visit to the police station for interrogation.

In an essay you wrote several years ago you discussed Valéry's famous sentence "The Marquise went out at five o'clock." Today, after writing a novel from which the Marquise is banished without a trace, how do you assess the genre as a vehicle for concerns of the spirit?

When I wrote that essay—it was exactly thirteen years ago—I was referring primarily to the French *nouveau roman* and the novelistic stutterings of Beckett's Molloy and trying to resist the temptation of "dehumanization." Here is what I said: "As an admirer of experiments and suffering and a supporter of revolt against convention, I draw the line at stammering, even if I am obliged to start my novel with the sentence: 'This morning I found human footprints in the sand.' "

Don't forget that at the time I hadn't published a single book and was gearing up to write a novel. I'd like to think that the footprints I spoke of then appear now in *Hourglass* and that from today's perspective the sentence they came from is almost magically prescient: the words *sand* and *human footprints* form the underlying metaphor, the very core and quintessence of *Hourglass*.

You write short stories and essays, novels and plays; you are a translator. Do you feel the wide range of genres at your command form a unity based on verbal expression, or are there experiences that require clear-cut genre boundaries?

The situation you brought to mind with your previous question—my having anticipated a novel in an essay— reveals even to me the way genres push and pull one another, interact. All my novels, especially *Hourglass*, include every aspect of my literary interests and experience: bits and pieces from essays, from ruminations on literary theory, remnants of poetic know-how acquired through translating verse and through early attempts at writing it, and perhaps something of the tension of writing for the stage—my whole literary heritage, all the genes of my reading and my involvement in literary activities of every kind.

While working on *Hourglass*, I tried to replace the monotony of a given style—the sort of thing a writer settles into after a long quest—with polyphony, a formal polyphony. Hence the use of the most varied literary devices—sometimes lyrical and sometimes essayistic, sometimes ironic and sometimes tragiserious, sometimes philosophical and sometimes parodical.

My ideal has always been a work that, after the first time round, can be read as an encyclopedia (the favorite reading material of Baudelaire and many others), by which I mean that it can be read for its sudden, giddy whirl of topics on the basis of chance and alphabetical (or some other) order, of lists of famous men and women together with thumbnail biographies—the lives of poets, scholars, politicians, revolutionaries, physicians, astronomers, and so on—superbly intermingled with the names of plants, in the vernacular and in Latin, the names of deserts, the names of ancient deities, the names of regions, the names of cities, with all the prose of the world. The analogies to be drawn, the laws of identity to be found!

In another interview we had a good eight years ago, you said you found "literature with a cause" ridiculous. How do you feel nowadays about commitment on the part of literature and the writer?

I was actually just rebelling against literary causes as conceived by Yugoslav writers, who tragicomically over-estimate their power and that of literature *hic et nunc*. On that occasion—and often thereafter—I brought up the fact that even Sartre, in conditions much more favorable to literature, expressed doubt in the power of a writer's commitment as such and opted for other ways of making his conviction felt: activism, journalism.

Then as now, my position comes from Krleža: people with "something to say" should leave literature alone and write for the papers. But no, they cram their petty grudges against this or that public figure into a novel and call it commitment, and whether it gets lost there like pressed flowers in a prayer book or blows up in their faces—both can and do happen—they take no responsibility: all they wanted was a little no-risk *engagement*.

Why then bother writing, you might ask. Let me try once more to give our drudgery meaning with a brief quotation from the critic Jean Ricardou: "Without the presence of literature, the death of a child anywhere in the world would be of no more import than the death of a beast in a slaughterhouse." Literature provides that death with a sense, a significance, a human weight, thereby al-leviating and ultimately overcoming it.

1973

Banality, Like
a Plastic Bottle,
Is Forever

*What prompted this conversation, I think, was more a desire to
have certain things clarified for myself—and therefore the reading
public—than to ask for a basic guide to what you have written.
As the old saw has it, writers shouldn't be asked to interpret
their work. Still, I'm interested in the clear-cut commitment in
your latest book,* A Tomb for Boris Davidovich. *It is so
strong as to make the work an all but scientific query after the
truth.*

I'm afraid you're in for a bit of a—no, more—a major
disappointment. My ideas are woven of skepticism; they
are skepticism itself. Their underlying principle might be
expressed as follows: don't believe anything anybody says;
everyone is a world unto himself, a lone planet, a star—
no, stardust—the grain of a meteor meeting other grains
by the blind laws of attraction and repulsion, colliding
stupidly, pointlessly; and speech, talk, is merely a source
of fresh misunderstanding. No one for whom speech and
ideas are not of the utmost importance (as they are, say,

for poets) has had or can have tragic misunderstandings with the world. Being a writer, says Andrić, "means putting a mound of printed paper and a mountain of vagueness and misunderstanding between yourself and others." Writing and speaking with this in mind is sheer torment, a form of masochism if you like: a writer could spend a lifetime (especially in Yugoslavia) reiterating basic statements and do nothing more than multiply misunderstandings. Of course, the problem lies not only in the semantic level, the level of meaning; there's also the deep-rooted mistrust of moral values on the part of philistines and journalists, the belief that writers are liars (which some are), that every written word is written with the intent of saying something other than what it says, that it says the opposite of what you, the writer, have written, and that there is a hidden (ideological or amoral) meaning behind every word. Even if they agree with you—with an idea you have clearly expressed—they still have plenty of opportunity to come down on you, either because they disagree with the way you've said it (which is fine) or because they think you should have written about something else.

Writers, unless they believe in God, are the loneliest people on earth—and the most misunderstood. By the way, don't expect me to clarify anything for you, let alone the "reading public." While we're having this abstract dialogue (and it *is* a dialogue), I can at least trust your curiosity, a curiosity composed of skepticism and faith in equal proportions, but all I can do for the "reading public" is add to the sum of misunderstandings (of which the very notion of a "reading public" is one), because all the "reading public" cares for is kitsch and cliché. So it's just the two of us.

(Maybe there are some others listening in, but they don't really grasp what we're saying; they're just waiting for us to fall into the trap of our misunderstandings so they can call in the police and the fire brigade. Well, let them.)

Who says writers shouldn't be asked to interpret their work? Let me tell you in all confidence: it's just another ruse dreamed up by our fire brigade, the tired old chestnut that writers are fools, ventriloquists who can somehow churn out novels but have no idea what they've done— only *critics* can know that, especially if the writers are dead or have their sights set on eternity and give critics free rein to interpret what they've said, chew it over and spit it out at reader and writer alike the way surgeons read a cardiogram or an X-ray of the chest or pelvis (especially the pelvis). Writers often take to these professional lies, these critical tea-leaf readings, because they discover to their astonishment and delight that their empty mumblings (in prose and verse) were actually about "Man" or "Alienation" or the "Crisis of Modern Society" and other such burning issues or all of them at once, so it never occurs to them to talk about their own opuscules except to praise them to the skies on the basis of critical acclaim. Writers thus believe in the authority of the critic: if the critic claims a work says such and such, the critic must be right; besides, a work of art has many meanings, many layers, multiple interpretations are de rigueur, paradoxes only make things more interesting. So writers admit loud and clear they're fools and ventriloquists or that it's all a matter of "inspiration."

But I say: beware of writers who don't know what

they've written and why; beware of writers who give you anecdote for reason. Either they're in cahoots with eternity (in which case they neither see nor hear you and stink of carrion before the fact) or they are in fact fools.

"The desire for truth" is nothing but a desire to avoid banality, and banality is immoral. It is immoral if it stems from ignorance and—especially—cowardice. In literature the banality that comes of ignorance gives rise to (or, rather, multiplies) uniformity, saps vital energy, creates rubbish dumps of clichés, and wastes paper. In a word, it's an ecological problem.

Banality, like a plastic bottle, is forever! The other type of banality, the banality of the coward, is also a banality of clichés, but one that conceals a lie: while waiting to be told what and when to attack, the coward is encouraged to keep up his lie, to fend off the moment of truth, of epiphany.

While writing my "family" novels, I left my readers to take me at my word; that is, I tried to seduce them with words, pass on certain childhood misgivings to them, certain tremors of early sorrows. All I had to rely on was artistic effect, the similarity of lineaments and landscapes, the well-known sense of recognition that gives music so much of its power. What I mean is that spells, incantations, *charges* (in Valéry's sense) were the only literary means I had to win over my readers, convince them that the words they were reading were not mere idle fantasies but a form of truth and experience. In *Hourglass*, where I switch to the third person and therefore lose the confessional tone, I was forced to use other devices (objective images, invented footnotes, "documents") so as to make readers believe, again, that they were reading more than fantasies or figments of the imagination, that they were reading the truth, and *not only artistic truth*. (I despise the breed of writer who produces compositions-on-command and with flowing hand and university degree pens prose or poetry for the order of the day or hour, for money, status, and fame; that is, a host of people who could have become doctors, engineers, bureaucrats, or firemen, which they usually still are, instead of idiots and social parasites.)

Truth, if only literary truth, is a type of commitment as long as a shadow of doubt hangs over every word. "The writer's job," Sartre says, "is to acquaint everyone with the world so no one can claim innocence." Writers must make us believe they know more than others yet doubt more than others.

In my most recent book I abandoned the realm of recognizable facts, the grid of values where the presence of a first-person narrator is enough to guarantee truthfulness and where memory, even as the key to the traumas of infancy, has lost its validity. The only points of connection, the only remaining links with my earlier books, are my style and certain mythic elements. The road I've taken is perfectly clear: from the first-person singular (in *Early Sorrows* and *Garden, Ashes*) to the third-person singular (in

Hourglass) to the third-person plural, them (in *A Tomb for Boris Davidovich*). Call it commitment if you like: an enlargement of the circle of reality as well as an increase in the obligations resulting from it, the need to come to grips with the period in question. All this puts limits on the use of the imagination. Even if you're writing about the Chaldeans, let alone a recent period and events whose eyewitnesses are still alive. What's more, the Stalinist period (which many historians in both East and West call a period of "historical necessity," as if speaking of a disastrous flood and implying a fateful reconciliation with destiny, a fateful victory) is still a matter of controversy, a phenomenon many historians are powerless—or unwilling—to explain, regarding it as if it were the Siberian meteorite whose inexplicable effects continue to breed the most outlandish hypotheses more than half a century after its discovery. A subject with such clear-cut historical and ideological implications, a subject tacitly off-limits (in both East and West) and therefore never aired openly—like death in petit-bourgeois society—not only forced me to immerse myself in the period, so mysterious and shrouded in secrecy (or distorted by the haze of propaganda), but also to shed any bias I might have had (except the bias of artistic sensitivity), to avoid "psychologizing" my characters, and to stick as closely as possible to the facts. That's probably what you had in mind when you talked about a "scientific query after the truth." Anyway, that's what was going through my mind as I worked on *A Tomb for Boris Davidovich*.

You have often said that "the effects of literature are invisible," but you seem to discount the very real effect it has on people:

transforming the way they look at things, raising their conscious-
ness. Why is there such fear of literature? Why has the written
word been so persecuted throughout history?

I mean several things when I call the effects of literature
"invisible." First, literature tries to make sense of an imperfect world and imperfect people. Like music, it yearns
for perfection, it yearns to give meaning to life and to
death. Cold comfort for us mortals, perhaps, but comfort
all the same. The invisible effects of literature are ethical
in nature or at least attempt to be so. The next thing I
meant was that writers are wrong to expect a direct result
from literature in terms of morals or ideology. Literature
is only a secondary manifestation of Hegel's world spirit,
Weltgeist, and as subject to psychoschizoid behavior as any
aspect of the human mind. Writing literature, even good
literature, does not necessarily link you to the absolute or
mean you're in the right. Not in the least. Over the last
fifty years, literature has been manipulated every bit as
much as other areas of the human spirit. And finally, if
you want to bring literacy to the people, the best thing
to do is become a village schoolmaster and write primers
and textbooks; they're much more effective than novels
and poems, a bona fide "direct influence." Like philosophy and ideology, literature as a field of knowledge cannot escape ambiguity, nor is it uniquely privileged. It may
raise consciousness; then again, it may not. All ideologies
know this just as they know how easily it can be bought
or crushed. Totalitarian ideologies always want to reduce
literature to a single dimension, channel it in a single direction, turn it into propaganda. "Greetings, comrade engineers of the soul" (Stalin).

All ideologies have explicit social programs whose unbendingly rational approach does not and will not allow for people who corrode each imperfection on the road to utopia with the acid of doubt. Hence the misunderstandings between poet and ideologue. Poetry is doubt. Ideology is the absence of doubt.

To what extent does the artistic style of an age express an inner need?

Writers can take one of three stands with respect to the age or period in which they live: they can be behind their time (in terms of world view, ideas, ideology, in other words in terms of style), they can be of their time, and they can be ahead of their time. In the first instance, the writer is a servant of ideology, a doddering graybeard aboard the tram of history, his false teeth gnawing through ideas once fresh and daring but now meaningless, ideas with nary a gleam of innovation or revelation. This is the most common stand: the writer as fossil-keeper of styles and ideas, forever multiplying the clichés of victorious ideologies, writing "in the name of mankind," writing "about and for mankind" (a mankind dead and gone, the remains of his youth), defending his works with an ideology and hiding behind it at the same time, a flatterer and a yes-man, who attacks anything and anybody young, novel, inventive, because he has discovered the definitive order of things and their perfection, he has found his style, a false and dangerous "humanism," in the name of which he destroys everything around him, pollutes it with his banalities, his perceptions of reality (half a century dead), a "man of principle," who refuses to change, who cares nothing for facts, being above and beyond them, above and beyond history and time, and if reality contradicts the ideas and ideals of his youth, he sticks to his guns with "terrifying consistency." Yes, amazingly enough, consistency is still the ultimate accolade in Yugoslavia: people who were and are Stalinists in spite of all that has come to light not only fail to don sackcloth and ashes, beg forgiveness for their misspent youths, and admit to having been led and misled, thus performing a dialectical *salto mortale* of confession and exculpation; they will declare in the spirit of German philosophy, "So much the worse for reality," and our audience will applaud them from the wings, from the darkness of the stalls, because they're consistent and there's nothing more honest than that.

So don't expect a Yugoslav writer to change in his fifties or sixties. No, he will continue to confirm his admirers' unconscious realization that their geniuses of consistency are in fact mummies and that they want nothing more of writers than that they should behave like mummies, thus placing them out of reach of the human and natural laws by which individuals and their conscience change as their knowledge and experience increase. Writers like these stand in the way of progress; they are fossilkeepers in the museum of a history that stopped for them with their youth (if they were ever young). Having found their "style" of thought, life, and art, they canonized it with the help of ideology, arms, and the fire brigade. "If you're against my poetry, you're against the Revolution!" Just try telling them their poetry isn't poetry (it's a fusty anachronism), that it isn't revolutionary (the Revolution has made a few dialectical about-faces since the canonization of their work, and they fail to notice that the tram of history has clanked on without them, that the tracks have been torn up, that they themselves are hovering in midair or even lying in the dust).

But, as I've said, writers can also be *of* their time, they can be its "antenna": they can have a finger on the pulse of the age, treat history as an evolution of ideas, a permutation of sensibilities, the thrust of Hegel's *Weltgeist*, and thus be capable of change and self-contradiction, of jumping down their own throats and recognizing yesterday's hopes as illusions. Or they can stand their guard, ears pricked, skepticism their only guide, never letting themselves or their work be canonized, always leaving space in the margins for corrections, additions, for the one big footnote to be filled in, if not before, then at the hour of their death, from the perspective of the future and by those able to recognize their errors or triumphs. For they were merely writers of their time and thus prone to every mortal failing (life membership in the National Academy notwithstanding).

The third type is the least common: writers ahead of their time, writers whose perfect pitch detects the tremors of history like the approach of a mighty earthquake, whose sensitivity registers phenomena in embryo, unaware though they may be that the shifts and stresses are barely perceptible to others. These are the greatest and rarest of writers; they stand with one foot in their time and the other in the future, like Beatrice's gentle lover, the frail troubadour unaware he was straddling two eras.

Not only can you not ask a writer to be a genius, you can't even tell a genius when you see one. So writers who are ahead of their time (we can only have the honor of having been their contemporaries) may well be invisible, unknown. Moreover, their work, looking as it does to the future, is a riddle and all contemporary criticism of it a guessing game—and a dangerous one at that: a work written *sub specie aeternitatis* must be judged *sub specie aeternitatis.*

What you *can* ask of writers—or at least hope for from them—is a clear explanation of their message to their contemporaries, even allowing for future adjustments. You must be able to distinguish the problems of the age in their work: it must be neither anachronistic nor (and this is more important) a passing fad dictated to order by the fashion of the moment nor a candidate for canonization. What I call modern is the style of the times, not its fashion but its quest, its questioning of all values, its realization (inherent in the work) that the world is changes, that ideas go out of date, that the style of the times is an obligation not to be ignored, because mildew and cobwebs will get you in the end, and no Academy, no glittering prizes, no ideological correctness will help you then.

To what extent do language and formal considerations influence the semantics of a literary text? (You have often made the point that what interests you most in a work of literature is form and thus language.)

When I pick up a book by one of our writers because someone has told me (or I've read in a review—even if only between the lines) it has "something to say," that is, something to say about things people don't like to talk about, I usually find myself up against a phenomenon that, if I'm not mistaken, is exclusive to Yugoslav writing. The writer in question has put down on paper what looks like an outspoken idea, an allusion to some politician or other, implicitly or explicitly engaging in ideological invective, expressing "discontent" or whatever, but behind the tongue-tied mass of cardboard figures and the "psy-chological" mess of their relationships, behind all the long-winded and semi-literate blather, what I see more often than not is that the outspoken idea is the petty po-lemic of a piqued hack who has decided to get something off his chest—usually long after the fact—by putting it in the form of a story or novel and showing his buddies he has "something to say." And if he's kept it under his hat for a while, well, now he hasn't received the pension he'd hoped for, so he's going to bring it out into the open and show them not only that he has something to say but that he can—or thinks he can—write. I must say I can't be bothered to work out whom the writer had in mind, the figures behind the "cutouts," because I find such literary creations unreadable, and for all their hidden polemics (which I can read about in the reviews if I so desire) they do not qualify as literature—they're just so much hot air, woozy ramblings in the mouths of marionettes, feeble-minded claptrap labeled prose and bound between covers. The best place for that kind of thing is the café or dive: I've heard analogous "outspoken ideas" and ideological revenge given far more appropriate form (the only appro-priate form, in fact) in the mouths of old drunks fueled by alcohol, their beautiful boozy tales embroidered with belches, tears, and the entire repertory of oral narrative—gestures and grimaces, brilliant curses and glorious lies—all of which has more artistic and literary value (because couched in the proper form, the oral narrative, and the proper context, a dive) than an alleged novel that the critics hint has "something to say."

There's many a slip twixt storytelling and the written word. It isn't enough to have "something to say" (as

Krleža tells us time and time again) or to have witnessed certain events or to be "honest" or "brave"; writing a book, writing a novel, takes something more. The gates of our literature (and I don't mean only the gates to our Writers' Association) should be inscribed with Sartre's maxim as motto, policy statement, and warning: "One does not become a writer because one has chosen to say certain things; one becomes a writer because one has chosen to say certain things in a certain way." Which means that if you have something to get off your chest, write a letter to the authorities or to a newspaper or put it down in the form of reminiscences or memoirs, so the editor can make the necessary emendations and the reader can follow the logic of your argument.

The problem is that neither critics nor readers in Yugoslavia are particularly interested in memoirs as a genre. When they are published, they are published in newspapers and, thus trivialized, usually ignored by critics. It is high time memoirs were given their due. To my mind, one of the best books in postwar Yugoslav literature is Karlo Štajner's memoirs of the gulag, *Seven Thousand Days in Siberia.* Just as I feel that barroom blather is the most appropriate format for "outspoken" ranting, so the memory is best served by memoirs, especially if they come from a witness who, though not a writer by calling, has a valuable, relevant store of experience beyond the everyday. With a bit of fortune, we might now have had a rich memoir tradition rather than a mass of pulp novels and novelettes. We have pulped a whole branch of literature, transformed noble experiences and bloodstained facts into penny dreadfuls, turned historical truth into puppet shows and waxworks.

It is the metaphysical level of meaning Roland Barthes has in mind when he claims that literature "must signify something other than its content and form, something that is its own conclusion, the thing that impresses us as literature" (to which Robert Escarpit would say, "It writes a state of history into the language"). This would seem to imply that literature cannot avoid commitment, a point I'd like to return to now.

The presence of the "metaphysical" is precisely what sets literature apart from the bulk of other written records and brings it close to music (no mean feat). At the same time it represents its most elusive aspect, its "musical soul"—invisible, irreducible, inexplicable, an unknown creating a third element out of two knowns, the Kirlianov Effect, something that goes beyond the senses and has more in common with parapsychology than psychology, though it can be recorded: David Faust (that's his real name!) has recently photographed "finger radiation." The "metaphysical radiation" or illumination of literature stumps all literary theory, whether it favors the biographical or social approach or (conscious of the Kirlianov Effect in literature) structuralist, formalist, and phenomenological approaches, which attempt to analyze the work, break it down into its atomic particles, reduce it to itself, its "essence." In this sense Barthes is right when he says, in the passage you quote, that literature "must signify something other than its content and form, something that is its own conclusion, the thing that impresses us as literature."

We have come now to the fine, intangible border separating literature from reportage and, similarly, literature that has a self-immanent quality—in other words, literature that has the grace of form and illumination—from literature that lacks it (though it may have a "metaphysical aura" about it); we have come to the point where no learned analyses can help either reader or critic, where no literary school is equal to the task, where no key will open the secret gates, where intuition, experience, and talent are our only guide. And talent, by definition, is what cannot be taught, what cannot be discovered by speculative methods, a sensitivity that, like the sense of hearing, we all have mysteriously built in (though perhaps in uneven measure). Can you imagine the braying that would ensue if someone put a tuning fork to the ears of certain of our critics and asked them to reproduce its pulsating pitch?

If literary criticism has brought us to this pass (not only here but throughout the world), to an eco-miracle of literature, the pollution of the literary environment with "perfect" products (a predicament even more striking in the visual arts), the main reason is that critical methodologies have proved barren in the face of the miracle that is the work of art. Criticism has fallen into the hands of people stranded halfway between art and theories of perception and convinced that by discovering a certain regularity and order in the domain of art they have discovered exact parameters for assessing it, thus committing the error positivism has committed in the fields of philosophy and anthropology.

True, writers haven't been sitting twiddling their thumbs either. Having learned from the critics that a work of prose or poetry is held together, like scaffolding or skeletons, by certain regularities, today's writers manage to act the part, imitate talent, assemble "structures," coherently and solidly built creations quite resembling the classical works of the spirit and using for the most part the language of today's philosophical and ethical discourse—alienation, dehumanization, the return to nature, Love, Death, the Absurd—all of which in terms of formal, linguistic features, in terms of the signifier and the signified, quite resembles the works where it is all immanent, works ablaze, yes, *ablaze* with these ideas (these and others), works radiating an invisible radiation that I cannot imagine will ever be photographed, not even in the negative ionic field of eighteen thousand volts used by our Faust to record his Kirlianov Effect. Though maybe if a new Faust aims his lens at the head of a sensitive reader reading two works in quick succession, two works similar in "structure" and written by two skilled writers on the same theme—maybe then a Faust Effect would show up on sensitive film in one instance while in the other the film would be blank, lack all trace of radiation or emotive echo.

But fortunately (or unfortunately)—fortunately at least for the pudding-headed writer-operators and their wheeler-dealer critic-managers—the Faust Effect would prove nothing, because even an "elegantly structured" excuse for a novel might well cause the aura to surround a scholar's learned cranium or a reader's hollow pumpkin of a skull (the resonator being the reading head, which sometimes echoes like a hollow pumpkin). And what is more normal than for people without talent to outnumber people with it and for people without ears that hear to outnumber people with them; what is more normal in this world of increasingly democratic science and education than for the external to develop at the expense of the internal, for form to dominate content (in an ontological sense), for content to be replaced by or confused with form? (The deception, I repeat, is more striking in the visual arts, but even there it's not easy to expose.) If there's something dangerous about the mass media, it's that they murder the "metaphysics" of a work, that they do not and cannot take account of metaphysical meaning(s), that they fail to nurture—worse, that they destroy—the ear. To say nothing of the soul.

1976

Seeking a Place
under the Sun
for Doubt

Only the bare outline of a family tragedy emerges from the following few words you once uttered in an interview: "My father disappeared in Auschwitz, as did his extended family." His letter dated April 5, 1942—first lost, then miraculously found—made you "stop as before an open pyramid or a manuscript pulled from the Dead Sea" and provided the impetus for one of your best novels, Hourglass. *In the preface to the French translation, Piotr Rawicz notes: "Kiš is a chronicler who never raises his voice, who writes in the same moderate tone about the commonplace and the tragic, and thus shows himself for what he is: a great poet." Where did you learn such mastery over yourself and your material? What experiences or artistic affinities fostered such apparent objectivity?*

If in interviews I have routinely neglected to mention certain pedestrian autobiographical data, it is not so much a matter of discretion as because facts like the disappearance of family members—the father, in my case—were until recently regarded as a typically Socialist Realist brand of biography and constituted an integral part of the classical Social Origins item—"What did you do and where were you during the war? Where were your parents and what did they do during the war?"—in application forms. The class you belonged to and the "rating" your parents scored served as a measure of your political loyalty, aesthetic support of Socialist Realism, and, in the last analysis, willingness to—how shall I put it—kowtow to public opinion and political forums. That is why until the recent "Birth Certificate,"* which I appended to my *Collected Works*,† I refrained from talking about family matters.

Then, too, the Auschwitz association could easily have pigeonholed me: I was afraid the label "Jewish writer" would stick. Any qualifier next to the noun "writer" diminishes its significance, its sovereignty, and I didn't want—nor do I want—to be a minority writer.

Even aside from all this—and here I come to the second part of your question—the fact remains that the Jews are the historical paradigm of our century. That, as much as painful personal experience, is what attracted me to Jewish themes. Nonetheless, I've always approached the subject with caution. I still do. Because I'm appalled at minority books, at the sectarian success they parade, at the minority alibi that gives them an extraliterary quality and makes the reader look at them differently. By the way, the reputation of certain Yugoslav writers rests entirely on this sort of sectarianism: they are first and foremost *Serb* or *Croat* (according to their programs) and only then writers: the adjective counts more than the noun. I want to escape the tyranny of the adjective.

If the only reason to read a book is that it deals with

---

* Appears in this volume, on page 3.
† *Djela Danila Kiša* (ten volumes), Zagreb/Belgrade, 1983.

blacks, Jews, homosexuals, or—sorry—women, then I'm not interested. I'd rather read an essay, a treatise, a documentary report. For a reverse example, take Proust: in Proust, the fact of "difference" is both secondary and primordial. And for positive examples of the Jewish motif in literature, take Kafka or Singer: they, too, put literature first, and the Jewish element makes itself felt primarily as a tragic view of life and the world. Moreover, it is counterbalanced—this tragic view of life—by a latent humor and the resulting irony.

On that basis, I approach being Jewish as a metaphor, which means I'm obliged to speak of it indirectly. Not that I do so exclusively for literary or aesthetic reasons. I also need to conceal the theme, mitigate its inherent tragic character and pathos. Here's an example of a "depatheticizing" metaphor from *Garden, Ashes*, my way of bringing across the fact that Eduard Scham wore the yellow star during the war: "He moved through the fields like a sleepwalker, lost in thought, waving his cane high in the air, following his star, which he would lose amid the sunflowers, only to find it again at the edge of the field on his greasy black frock coat."

I've always given biographical and autobiographical facts the "weight" (formalistically speaking) of metaphor and irony. That is what makes them literature.

The final part of my question was about the artistic affinities that fostered your objectivity.

I believe objectivity comes from the use of metaphor, which means that objectivity is also a consequence of artistic experience. And artistic affinities, of course. Because, paradoxical as it sounds, concealing the theme leads to objectivity. As does the resulting irony. And all that comes from artistic idiosyncrasies on the one hand and affinities on the other.

Do you mean that stylistic devices let you forget your life, exclude your self?

My awareness of the latent danger of grandiloquence, sentimentality, and pathos serves as an ever-present form of self-censorship. The result is that I objectify life and cultivate an ironic attitude vis-à-vis my own (latent) lyricism.

Before Garden, Ashes *you wrote a novel entitled* Psalm 44, *a novel with a very concrete theme: Auschwitz. The sign "Für Juden verboten" (No Jews Allowed) occurs several times in the text. It would be hard to call* Psalm 44 *a metaphor. Even in the interviews you gave in 1973, when you won the NIN Prize for Literature, you avoided mentioning its theme. I have a feeling you wanted to avoid pronouncing the word* Auschwitz. *That's another kind of concealment.*

Exactly. *Psalm 44*, I must say, was a work of my youth, though I don't repudiate it (I've included it in my *Collected Works*), because if nothing else it provides a kind of continuity with my later works. By now the connection between *Psalm 44* and, say, *A Tomb for Boris Davidovich* should be perfectly plain: both deal with—how shall I put it?—violence or, more precisely, the camps—the former with the Nazi camps, the later with the Soviet camps (which are sometimes given the shameful euphemism of Stalinist).*

But let's go back to the work itself. Even in that first

---

* Prior to his death, Kiš decided not to permit any new, separate editions or translations of *Psalm 44*.

short novel I tried to avoid pathos by using various literary devices such as "lyrical defamiliarization." But what bothers me to this very day is that despite it all, despite the lyrical admixture, I said certain things directly—things like "*Für Juden verboten*"—for want of literary experience. Now I know I'd find other, more felicitous solutions to the problem. I found them in my later works, which in a way are actually corrections of, emendations to, *Psalm 44* and that egregious—from my standpoint, at least— literary error. Yet much as it rests on my own experience and the testimony of those few relatives who returned from the camps, even *Psalm 44* belongs to the genre of the documentary because its plot goes back to a newspaper story about a Jewish couple and their child several years after the war visiting the camp where the child was born.

When I wrote the book—it was ages ago, I was about twenty-five—I felt the time had come to liberate myself from certain war-related themes weighing heavy on me, but they were completely at odds with the way Yugoslav literature had portrayed the war not only thematically but also stylistically. That may explain the shame I felt when talking about the book, a shame I still feel in a way. I also believe that the presence of a latent resistance to Jewish subject matter in the context of Yugoslav reality was instrumental in my search for what I call my own literary metaphor.

What do you mean when you say "Yugoslav reality"? That people didn't talk about the fate of the Jews? Or is it more a personal thing, a kind of pride on your part, an "I don't want to be seen as a victim" attitude?

Like it or not, being Jewish is an exceptional *condition humaine* and one that—regardless of time, place, or social system—has negative consequences for whoever happens to be marked by it. It is an issue unfailingly broached with discomfort and from a Manichaean perspective, either with hypocrisy or with sensitivity (which I, too, invariably share). I have been—and am to this day—subject to certain psychological inhibitions, and since I consider my fate to be primarily that of a writer, I have tried to transform these negative factors into what you might call positive literary ones. What I mean is I have concealed the Jewish component in my literary works. I was equally afraid of the weight of fact, which is dangerous for literature, and of the possibility of becoming or being taken for a minority writer. And the danger of pathos and grandiloquence is latent in all "minority literatures."

You've said somewhere that you came up with the idea for A Tomb for Boris Davidovich *in Bordeaux, that it originated as a reaction to the talks and arguments you had with your students and colleagues.*

I lived in Bordeaux in the seventies, a time of leftist enthusiasm in France and the West in general, when the facts about the Soviet camps were not yet accepted. It mustn't be forgotten that even though Solzhenitsyn's *Gulag Archipelago* appeared about then, leftist intellectuals not only refused to accept the horrible fact of Soviet camps —whose existence is one of the central facts of our age —but refused even to read it, considering it an act of ideological sabotage and right-wing conspiracy. Since it was impossible to discuss anything on the level of general ideas with them—they had a priori, aggressive attitudes about everything—I felt obliged to formalize my arguments in the form of anecdotes and stories based on Solzhenitsyn himself and Karlo Štajner, Eugenia Ginzburg, Nadezhda Mandelstam, Roy Medvedev, etc. These anecdotes were still the only form of conversation they were ready to accept or, rather, listen to. Because, when it came to ideology, sociology, or politics, they brooked no opposition, those alleged intellectuals; they were extremely intolerant and saw everything in Manichaean terms: the East was heaven, the West was hell—exploitation, consumerism, etc., etc.

Was that the position of your Slavicist colleagues or of others as well?

It was the general tone of the French intelligentsia, in Paris as well as in Bordeaux; it was the general tendency —if you don't mind my saying so—of the Western intelligentsia as a whole. The gulag didn't fit their facile schemas, and they preferred closing their eyes to confronting Soviet camps. Today they are just as belatedly discovering the existence of Chinese camps and the millions of victims of the Great Leap Forward.

Let me quote from your essay "Paris, Great Kitchen of Ideas": "I dislike hearing Paris intellectuals cite the same names ad nauseam—Marx, Freud, Mao, Sartre—and never or almost never Montaigne, Baudelaire, Flaubert, Camus." Obviously you were generalizing from a small circle of writers—if you were referring to writers, that is. I find it hard to believe that all French intellectuals fit the pattern you describe. I'm certain there are writers who have no interest in fashionable political ideas, who shrink from them.

Let me add Lacan to my list, and Marcuse, Lukács . . . Examine it closely and you'll see it has a Marxist bias to it, the Marxist line having been until recently—and to some extent until today—the only valid one for the French intelligentsia. Thinkers who brought up other names and cultivated doubt—Montaignian doubt—and lucidity, thinkers like Raymond Aron in France or Arthur Koestler and Karl Popper in England, not only failed to be heard but were rejected *en bloc* and a priori as reactionaries, bourgeois intellectuals, "fascists." Even when the intellectual terror began to weaken, the French intelligentsia was for the most part silent. No, the example I gave was no exaggeration; it was simply a statement of fact.

You say in your Homo Poeticus *that the change in direction, in fashion, can be partly attributed to certain* nouveaux philosophes. *Which ones had you in mind?*

First let me dissociate myself from the word *fashion*: it's too weak; it implies a kind of justification and, innocent as it sounds, it was the word used by the intellectual terrorists themselves. Fashion is harmless, while that was fanaticism, blindness, and arrogance.

As for the *nouveaux philosophes*, I had in mind primarily André Glucksmann and Bernard-Henri Lévy. They played the part of translators or interpreters by preparing a kind of digest of Solzhenitsyn, Aron, Koestler, and Popper for the average reader, that is, by offering the French public a new set of insights (new to the French) and sowing the seeds of doubt in what had been solid, impervious ideological ground. The reason *they* had to be the ones to play the role was that according to the egocentrism typical of the French character only a Frenchman can communicate even the plainest facts from the world of ideas to the French reader; otherwise, they have no weight. Another thing that helped to popularize the ideas was the fact that most of the *nouveaux philosophes* had been leftists—Communists and Maoists (in the same person)—and their leftist past was taken as proof of their good intentions.

"How can we doubt the wonders of science," you state somewhere sarcastically. *"When a new Dr. Barnard transplants a pig's heart into us, we'll be able to grunt like pigs. And when we're all grunting with our pig hearts, the last humans who still see with human eyes will be those for whom the experience of art was not alien."*

What I meant to say was that most people live hideously happy lives (a chance oxymoron, that) in their *sancta simplicitas* and their profound faith in science. Science with a capital S, confident it can cure all ills. And then I thought about the destruction of philosophy in the name of science, of the philosophy that didn't claim to be a science but only a reflection on the human condition—where do we come from? who are we? where are we going?—on life and death, "the last things," on what Camus formulated, after the Greeks, as the most basic issue in all philosophy, the issue of suicide. With the coming of the twentieth century all metaphysical questions were swept away by a universal wave of materialism and Marxism, and the philistine and the intellectual along with the peasant from television's "global village" are equally convinced that there is no more mystery, that science, history, and progress have solved all our problems.

All but one: the problem of human immortality. But now that a pig's heart or a baboon's heart has been transplanted into a human chest, immortality is just around the corner! Now we know the reason for historical evolution from the low to the high. The great equation has been solved scientifically and comes out even. Hence no more mystery, no more doubt.

The only people still filled with wonderment at the equation and the mystery of the starry firmament are the poets among us. Only they inject anxiety and doubt into the general confidence; only they look beyond heart transplants and bodies frozen for eternity to the problem of life and death. That's more or less what I meant when I remarked ironically that I was seeking a place under the sun for doubt; that is, literature and art; that is, poets. Science and history cannot take the place of poetry.

In the same text you say you can't love Paris if only because "it has no ear for Andrić, Krleža, or Crnjanski," writers you regard as your masters.

I don't want my love-hate relationship with Paris reduced to one objection: I have many others. The reason I brought up those three writers, the reason I bring them up elsewhere in my writings, is to provide myself with a —how shall I put it?—family. All writers have ancestors, and if they haven't—as Borges says—they must create them. If you tell a Frenchman (and not only a Frenchman) that you are, say, a Russian writer, he knows at once where to place you because he knows, in a manner of speaking, your family: if you're a Russian writer, you belong—automatically, by inheritance—to the great family of Gogol, Tolstoy, and Chekhov. You're not a stranger; you've got an identity.

But we of the lesser languages and literatures (a category that includes more than Yugoslav writers—Dutch writers, for instance) must always identify ourselves, list our forebears. By bringing up names of Yugoslav writers, I wish to inform the Western reader I'm not without roots, I'm not an orphan. Though I'm afraid the Western reader will find it hard to grasp what we mean by looking for our roots, and if I bring up these three, it's not only because I believe them to be great European writers but also because, unlike many French writers, they took literature seriously and experienced it tragically.

Some critics liken you to Borges when discussing A Tomb for Boris Davidovich. *Would you formulate again to what extent it was a polemic with Borges and to what extent Borges served as a stimulus for the work.*

As I've said before, I believe Borges took a revolutionary step forward in the art of storytelling by combining some of its most interesting modern technical innovations: Poe's intriguing plot lines, for example, and the use of documents both genuine and bogus (for this he had something of a predecessor in Marcel Schwob), which gives the story a kind of double twist: the reader is reading the story naïvely on the level of content, subject matter, and the writer is inventing and inserting a document so as to create the impression that the story is more than convincing, that the story is true. What attracted me most to Borges was his new way of using "documents." It enabled him to compress his material to the maximum, which is, after all, the ideal of narrative art. I repeat: the document is the surest way to make a story seem both convincing and true, and what is literature for if not to convince us of the truth of what it tells, of the writer's literary fantasies. Such is the direction Borges's investigations take, and they lead him to the pinnacle of narrative art and technique. According to Shklovsky's classic formulation, a writer inherits the sum total of the technical possibilities of the age. All writers, not just Borges. Shklovsky's formulation is paradigmatic of the art of narration and literature as a whole when it says: Don't be a dilettante and don't be anachronistic.

I recognize some of the arguments you used in the polemics surrounding A Tomb for Boris Davidovich.

Certain misunderstandings connected with *A Tomb for Boris Davidovich* arose from a failure on the part of the Yugoslav critics to understand that in this sort of literature "sources" mustn't be revealed. If I'd revealed my sources, I'd have upset the whole structure of the fiction, because when true and false quotations are mixed together, identifying the former lays bare the latter.

How much was *A Tomb for Boris Davidovich* a polemic with Borges? I was convinced from the start, from the first words I wrote, that the polemic was so plain that both critics and the common reader would have no trouble seeing what I was up to; I thought my appropriation of the Borgesian model made it obvious I was polemicizing with him (since we always take a polemical stand vis-à-vis our models). I turned out to be wrong.

The polemic consists in the following: Borges calls his most famous book *A Universal History of Infamy*. On the thematic level, however, it's not a "universal history of infamy" but—I repeat, on the thematic level—a collection of children's stories with no social relevance whatsoever, stories about New York gangsters, Chinese pirates, backwoods highwaymen, and suchlike. So I directed my polemic primarily against his title, which goes much too far (as he himself later admitted). I claim that the universal history of infamy is the twentieth century and its camps —Soviet camps, most of all. Infamy is when in the name of the idea of a better world for which whole generations have perished, in the name of a humanistic idea, you build camps and conceal their existence and destroy both people and their most intimate dreams of that better world. The universal history of infamy therefore includes the destiny of all the unfortunate idealists who left Europe for the "Third Rome," Moscow, and were shamelessly lured into a trap, where they bled and died like animals.

The idea behind *A Tomb for Boris Davidovich* came from the convergence of two points: my experience with Western intellectuals who unreservedly supported the infamy of history and Borges's totally unsuitable title. Maybe the reason why so few readers have discovered my polemic with Borges is that, as Borges himself maintains, there are fewer good readers than there are good writers. And I would add: fewer good critics than good readers.

In an essay dated 1960 you state: "As an admirer of all adventures of the spirit and rebellions of the mind and heart, I am full of admiration for anyone who despises the sentence 'The Marquise went out at five o'clock,' yet I am convinced that there is more art and more life in that sentence than in a muffled crunch of sand with no human footprints and no human voice: as an admirer of experiments and suffering and a supporter of revolt against convention, I draw the line at stammering, even if I am obliged to start my novel with the sentence: 'This morning I found human footprints in the sand.' " Would you explain what you had in mind?

When I used the word *stammering*, I was thinking principally of certain Yugoslav literary experiments in both poetry and prose, but I was also doffing my hat to Joyce and thinking of his "glorious defeat," as Virginia Woolf once referred to *Ulysses*. Because Joyce is certainly the one who revealed to us modernists how far a writer can experiment and at what cost. Incidentally, I recently read that near the end of his life Joyce was asked the direction he would have taken if he'd been able to start again from scratch, and what he said was, "Simplicity."

Of course, finding a form for prose is not so matter-of-fact as all that. Literature demands to be different; it is always on the lookout for maximal solutions, solutions that encompass as much as possible of the totality of the world and its phenomena and avoid the banality of the common, philistine point of view. That is why it strives for what the Russian formalists called *ostranenie*, defamiliarization, which can also be achieved through a "zero degree of writing" and other formal devices. Discoveries occur on both sides. As do defeats, of course.

Experience, however, has taught me that all formal innovation involves a risk of misunderstanding on the part of the reader, that even the most straightforward instance of defamiliarization or the use of a new device, a new way of viewing reality, causes misunderstandings, to say nothing of a consciously experimental work, one that oversteps the commonly accepted bounds of literature.

Can you be more specific?

Let me take an experiment that is related in a way to

my experience, the French *nouveau roman*. In their theoretical works the writers of the school have pointed to
weaknesses in classical realistic literature and the hack-
neyed quality of its devices, but in their literary works
they have failed to justify their theoretical premises. Even
so, I believe that many contemporary writers—myself
included—have derived real benefits from their experiments. I have in mind the rejection of the literary type
and of psychology as the basic driving force in the novel.

*In a 1982 text you say, "I dislike using a subject matter or
approach more than once. I absolutely must have both an obsessive theme and a change of register—change of key, to put it in
musical terms—and not merely from work to work but even
within a work, within a story." The theme of death runs like a
leitmotiv through your most recent work,* The Encyclopedia of
the Dead. *The stories that constitute it differ stylistically among
themselves and are all based on existing sources—apart from the
title story, which you "heard," and "Red Stamps with Lenin's
Picture," which you "made up." Moreover, the two stories in
question share a formal characteristic: they are told in the feminine
first-person singular. What does this "change of register" mean
in the creative process? To what extent is a morphological or
syntactic form the driving force for the mechanism that imposes a
new device and with it a content not even the writer may suspect?*

To answer the first part of your question, *Hourglass* is
my most striking example of variations on a theme: it
consists of four separate, alternating "manuscripts." I
wrote it in a number of registers or, rather, pushed on for
some two or three hundred pages in one and stopped
because I didn't enjoy playing in one register and at the
same tempo—andante, say—on the typewriter for hours
and days at a time. I need to switch registers, go from

major to minor and back again, from legato to staccato, from lyrical or poetic passages to essayistic ones. In *A Tomb for Boris Davidovich* I also intersperse essay-like chapters with lyrical digressions. The central story, the one with the fourteenth-century subject matter (the whole of which is more or less a word-for-word quotation), serves primarily, above and beyond the plot level, as a register change.

Register change is plain in *The Encyclopedia of the Dead* as well. When you try out a motif on paper, you've got to find the best possible device for it, one that won't work for another motif or story. This permanent search for form is characteristic of all modern, not to say "decadent," writers. Nineteenth-century writers were different: once they had found a basic stylistic technique, they stuck to it. Then came Flaubert and the breakdown in values. Flaubert was the first to call their ideal project into question and look for new stylistic answers. An "age of doubt" had dawned, and doubt led to searching, the final product of which, of course, was Joyce. Clearly Joyce's development from *Dubliners* through *Ulysses* to *Finnegans Wake* is a painful illustration of the search for absolute form. And although the constant questioning not only of form but of literature itself during the composition of a story or novel is the hallmark of modern fiction, a Western publisher, given the Western publishing industry, would probably beg me to write a second, third, and fourth book on a "similar theme" to *A Tomb for Boris Davidovich* without changing my style or technique.

Would you do it?

Of course not, not for anything. But that's basically how it is in the publishing world of the consumer society:

both publisher and reader expect you to repeat what they know, varying your subject matter somewhat but preserving your language, your trademark. Luckily I can rest easy on that score; I am at leisure to seek out new themes and techniques from book to book with a clear conscience. And only if they obsess me. I can't sit down and write on order, in response to the demands of the market. Even if I am a professional writer, I write only when I must, when I'm driven by an inner need, when I'm beyond indulging my sloth or love of creature comforts. And once I'm at the typewriter, I have to keep myself entertained by the "production process." Hence the need for variety and change of register.

My use of women narrators in those two stories from *The Encyclopedia of the Dead* is also the result of a quest for change, for a new psychological register and a new voice.

Part of my question had to do with the function of documents in that book.

Right. You say all the texts are based on existing sources, and I say the stories that most resemble documents contain the most fiction. Because—the "Postscript" notwithstanding—that's where the imagination predominates. Making your readers believe in the truth of your story, making them believe that what they are reading actually happened, that, I repeat, is the main goal of every work of literature. Any means to that end is acceptable as long as it works. The main function the documentary method serves is to convince readers of the authenticity of both the story and the "document" the writer has offered them. What is true and what is false, what is a genuine document and what is a forgery—that is, a document modeled after a genuine one—is neither here nor there. All that matters is convincing the reader, conveying the illusion of truth. Handing the reader the key to the puzzle would mean destroying the illusion you have been at pains to create. As Borges put it, there's no point in giving too many hints because they increase the reader's attention to detail and thus detract from the aesthetic experience. A crucial point. Source-hunting should be left to the critic, primarily the academic critic: it may lead to fascinating results.

In The Anatomy Lesson *you bring up Shklovsky in this regard.*

Yes, Shklovsky's *Material and Style in Leo Tolstoy's "War and Peace,"* in which he shows how a document "reflected" through a work of art undergoes a transformation and can be misused. What did Tolstoy actually do? He made history over after his own design; that is, he used documents to write his own tendentious story of the fatherland's war, turning the Battle of Borodino into a triumph for the Russian Army, which it was not, and Napoleon into a rag doll and clown, which he was not. He said nothing about the heroism of the French soldiers; he said nothing about how Russian civilians massacred the disarmed, retreating French military (because he ignored part of the documents); he said nothing about—or "falsified" (I put the word *falsified* in quotes because writers have the right to use documents in accordance with their judgment and conscience)—the pro-Napoleon sentiment among certain strata of the population; and so on and so forth. As a result, *War and Peace* is poorer than the sources it is based on: the war was bloodier, crueler, and much less Manichaean than Tolstoy's nationalist, officer-corps reconstruction of it. In this sense Tolstoy might be seen as the first Russian writer to use what the Russians themselves call *lakirovka* (the technique of whitewashing reality) and even as a forerunner of Socialist Realism. Shklovsky's analysis makes it clear that the documentary method— and montage technique as well—can be as easily misused as an approach arrived at by the free play of the imagination. If Tolstoy had been more veracious in his use of documents and memoirs, the potential *War and Peace* could have surpassed even the masterly *War and Peace* we have. But now we are in the realm of speculation.

Let's go back to The Encyclopedia of the Dead. *The title story speaks of the encyclopedia as an ideal text: it sees history as the sum of human destinies, the totality of ephemeral happenings often condensed into a single paragraph. Might not such a paragraph be analogous to a consciousness that spends all its time gathering a multitude of facts and bringing them together in a configuration it finds congenial?*

Every consciousness aspires to an ideal formula. Einstein's formula is merely the end product of his speculations. And even though the fields are different, I believe a writer aspires to press the greatest possible experience into the least possible space. What is a line of poetry other than an attempt, a constantly repeated attempt, to condense the essence of an intuition or feeling into a single sentence, an ideal formula? Take the Japanese haiku, which compresses the ideal expression of a lyrical experience into a few lines, or its more unwieldy, more baroque Western counterpart, the sonnet.

When I describe *The Encyclopedia of the Dead* as a meeting place for all human events, I mean it as a metaphor for my own poetics in an ideal, unattainable form. It's a description of an ideal project of condensation, the final product of which is the story "The Encyclopedia of the Dead," which is in fact a condensed novel, a novel reduced to some forty pages. I might add that another writer, less indolent and with a different poetics, would doubtless have turned the same material into a full-fledged classical, nineteenth-century-like psychological novel, something a lot fatter than, say Maupassant's *Une vie*, but what I wanted to do was compress the substance of a novel into a short story.

I believe that in its ideal, unattainable, Platonic form the novel should resemble an encyclopedia entry or, rather, a series of entries branching out in all directions yet condensed. This view comes from long years of reveries on the subject of encyclopedias, which I've always thought of as a treasure trove of material for the novel. If you stick to the old-fashioned—and obviously inaccurate—formula that calls a novel "the life of a person from the cradle to the grave," the most succinct novel would be an epitaph, a tombstone inscription giving name and dates of birth and death.

By the way, the desire to be succinct makes itself felt in my other works as well. Hence their brevity, fragmentary character, frequent changes in register, and so on.

Could you say something about the function of quotations in your work? You use them often, both made up, invented—as you say—and real. Krleža also made frequent use of quotations. Let me cite an example from his Trip to Russia *that reminds me of how you use them. "Russian sleeping cars are wider and more comfortable than international ones; there is tea available, and the laundry rooms have hot running water to 'wash away the spilt blood' " and so on.*

Is it a quotation? I don't believe the original 1925 edition had that sentence about the spilt blood . . . Anyway, the first time I read the book, when I was sixteen or seventeen, I didn't know what I knew about Soviet reality when I reread it two years ago—things Krleža knew even then. Or at least suspected. It's interesting in light of all this that in *A Trip to Russia* the only negative figure among the Russians is a former Imperial admiral, whom Krleža assigns the role of informer: in his programmatic view of things at the time, the Revolution's dirty deeds could not be done by a "new man."

The main thing a quotation does is to let you say something that would otherwise seem banal and unconvincing. But it also functions as a form of defamiliarization. The writer discovers phenomena in reality which seem so out of the ordinary that no creative imagination could have hit upon them; the very fact that they are out of the ordinary makes them literary: they have been "defamiliarized" by reality. In such a situation the writer has no choice but to take them straight from reality.

Here's an example I recently came across in the papers. One of those little principalities—Andorra, I think it was—turns out to be the world's biggest producer of— guess what? Put yourself in the shoes of a writer who's describing the tiny country where the action of his novel takes place and who for an ironic touch needs two unusual articles produced by the country. When I ask writers to come up with something, they go on and on until I tell them what I found in the newspaper: it's the world's biggest producer of—false teeth and synthetic sausage skins! No literary imagination could possibly have come up with better examples, and no writer worth his salt would fail to take advantage of them.

But what if a writer did come up with them or something similar?
Even if you came up with something equally bizarre—and I doubt you would—you wouldn't dare use it. I wouldn't, anyway, for the simple reason that it would sound whimsical, unconvincing, farfetched. The moment I know it's a fact, however, it starts feeling plausible and I can use it without compunction in spite of, or even because of, its bizarre quality. In other words, a quotation is an anchor that holds the imagination fast to reality, keeps it down to earth. Prose is an earthbound creation, after all; it grows in the ground like a potato. (Poetry is a different matter.)

1984

Naming Is
Creating

Is it wanting to write that makes the writer?

No one comes to writing by accident. The first and most important stimulus is the treachery of biography, and the mechanism that triggers the imagination in a biography is an overwhelming sense of difference, the "shameful stigma" of difference. By trying to explain the origins of our difference and its relation to the world, we writers or future writers question our existence, and in so doing we take the most decisive step toward literature, which, as Barthes has said, entails just that: asking questions of ourselves.

This difference you mention—what does it consist of?

As a Jew or half-Jew in fascist Hungary (it made no difference), I was humiliated on a daily basis; I lived a life of fear, hunger, and injustice. Don't forget I saw the world through the eyes of a child and was therefore lacking in the philosophical, historical, and logical concepts to ex-

plain my situation and account for the misfortunes afflicting me and my family. I took it all to be a natural calamity
(like a forest fire, flood, or bolt of lightning) and gave the
maelstrom a metaphysical interpretation: I saw the hand
of the Old Testament God at work.

Was that your "first step" toward literature?

We obviously feel the need—I felt the need—to work
out the reasons for God's wrath (though later I came to
see that God had nothing—or precious little—to do with
it, that the source of our misery was all too human); I
needed to find reasons for the ordeal that cost me my
father. It's the kind of inheritance that marks you for life.
No change of place or time can efface the stigma of difference. Not even returning to Yugoslavia, returning
home. If there's a mystery no one can escape and not even
free will can solve, it's the mystery of the "Wandering
Jew." Even if I'd obeyed my mother—who in the will
of sorts she made before she died insisted I burn all documents connected with my father—I wouldn't have escaped my fate: becoming a writer.

Marked by the taint of "cosmopolitanism" (with its
special East European connotations), "dissident and stateless," I was obliged by force of circumstance to find my
roots and title of nobility in literature. And if my claim
to "nobility" is more valid than most, it is because the
motto on my coat of arms would read with Baudelaire:
"Pain is my only nobility."

*You mention documents in connection with your father. What
part do they play in your work?*

I distrust the arbitrariness of the imagination—it is my

greatest literary obsession—and I question more than psychology, undermined as it is by the moderns and the *nouveau roman*; I question the very concept of literature.

I believe that literature must correct History: History is general, literature concrete; History is manifold, literature individual. History shows no concern for passion, crime, or numbers. What is the meaning of "six million dead"(!) if you don't see an individual face or body—if you don't hear an individual story?

Literature corrects the indifference of historical data by replacing History's lack of specificity with a specific individual. And how can I correct History through literature, how can I make up for History's indifference if not by using authentic documents, letters, and objects bearing the traces of real beings.

Literature is the concretization of abstract History. Documents are indispensable because if we rely exclusively on the imagination we run the risk of slipping back into abstraction.

You use documents to confirm historical reality in both Hourglass *and* A Tomb for Boris Davidovich, *don't you?*

Documents and eyewitness reports. An eyewitness report is the best document. For its naked power, for what it says and, even more, for what it fails to say, the spaces between words and sentences. The father's letter in *Hourglass* and Karlo Štajner's testimonies in some of the stories in *A Tomb for Boris Davidovich* give the works the seal of truth and set limits to the imagination without fettering it. On the contrary. They turn literature into what Claude Lanzmann calls "a fiction of reality."

*Much as you make of the "horrors of History," you never name
them.*

Even talking to you now, I'm reluctant to name them.
The victim is in a position of weakness and mortification.
I'd be displaying my stumps or scars, as it were, which is
equally distasteful to the displayer and the beholder. Refusing to name them gives them dignity. What I write
isn't meant to make anyone feel guilty; it's meant to provide a kind of catharsis. For me the unnamed victim is
the greatest victim of History. In my works the Jew is the
symbol of all the pariahs of History. To name is to dimin-
ish.

Here my position approaches that of the symbolists,
who preferred suggesting to naming because naming de-
prives the reader of half the pleasure: "One must never
quite conceive the idea as such."

Obviously, this makes for almost insoluble problems.
How can I describe a bygone time and world that others
feel obliged to represent by salient features and obvious
tags and symbols? How can I evoke a Star of David without displaying it? Well, the Star of David becomes a sun-
flower on Eduard Scham's frock coat. And Stalin, for
Boris Davidovich, is the portrait on the wall of the inter-
rogator's office or the name of a boat passing through a
canal dug by gulag prisoners.

*Your reference to Baudelaire is paradoxical. How can you speak
of suffering and avoid pathos?*

I have the same problem there as with naming. How
can I speak objectively of suffering? How can I use irony,
the basic weapon against pathos, without sounding cynical? Poetry and pathos are too often confused, and prose

demands the opposite of pathos: the effect must reside less in the text than in the reader's mind, in images.

But isn't an image in itself a poetic device?

All I mean by images is the concrete as opposed to the conceptual. Rhetorical figures serve only to transform the author's poetic or lyrical feeling into a dense text with none of the feeling that inspired it, to achieve what the Russian formalists call "defamiliarization" and "weighted form."

Would you say something about the importance of enumeration as a device?

Enumeration is primarily the reduction of objects to the spitting image of the world. Naming is creating.

I've always been fascinated by the diversity of things. Long ago I wrote a poem that was nothing but a detailed inventory of the contents of a trash can, the résumé of a world, the simplest of résumés. The remains of any object conceal a story, and more often than not I prefer naming objects to telling their story: the trash can has its archaeological layers.

Reading the Bible, Homer, or Rabelais, I keep finding devices engendered by the disparity and incongruity of objects in chance encounter. If I hadn't been amazed by the same sort of jumble as a child, I don't think I'd have been able to recognize enumeration as a literary device; without the autobiographical underpinning, I might have dismissed it as an arbitrary game.

The trash can, like the cemetery, is a great repository of the world, its very essence. Random juxtaposition makes for strange and wonderful combinations. As in Lautréamont's formula.

Is that where the Bus, Ship, Rail, and Air Travel Guide *in* Garden, Ashes *comes in?*
The timetable is the trash can of cities writ large; it is a sort of Cabala, the title of nobility I was speaking of. Which makes me the son of a "writer," of an authentic wanderer and traveler from Kakania.

Your story "The Encyclopedia of the Dead" in the book of the same name resumes and develops the obsession with the Book that characterizes Garden, Ashes.
The encyclopedia described in the story is both, as you say, an obsession with the Book and the consequence of a purely technical problem: how to introduce cultural, literary, and even philosophical references into the biography of an ordinary person, an individual; in other words, how to raise the "narrative horizon" of a literary character with a limited cultural horizon, how to attribute a part of one's own cultural heritage to a fictitious being. The solution I came up with was to make the character a figure in an encyclopedia or, to be more precise, an encyclopedia entry, which was in itself a cultural act. In so doing I was also able to condense the contents of a life into a series of data, images, and figures from a definite time and place: Yugoslavia from 1910 to 1970. In this way the material of an entire classical novel of the "life story" genre became a relatively short story and has, I hope, gained in density as a result. I wasn't playing literary games or being lazy; the work stems from a profound conviction that an abridged or condensed form, a form under tremendous

intellectual pressure, engenders a content rich in new meanings and an almost philosophical tension.

Are you one of the archivists of the mythical Library of Babel?

"The Encyclopedia of the Dead" obviously came from the shelves of the illustrious Argentine, because, according to his own account, his library contains all the books in the world. Though "in that library no two books are the same."

Anyway, from that vast quantity of books, from that memory of the world, I chose a picture book which, since I could not reproduce it, I merely described and glossed. Perhaps the Librarian failed to include it in his vast collection because it struck him as unimportant and childish and he preferred philosophical works or at least encyclopedias dealing with people known for their minds or crimes.

But the library also contains a book that is far less naïve, the book you call "The Book of Kings and Fools."

The story you mention, as I explain in the "Postscript" to *The Encyclopedia of the Dead*, is an abridged version of the birth of *The Protocols of the Elders of Zion*; that is, the history of a book whose origins and consequences are "fantastic," but lethally so. My literary fantasy followed a course that was the mirror image of Borges's: with him, crime became book; with me, book caused crime. What fascinated me in the genesis and destructive consequences of *The Protocols* was its totally unique literary and fantastic side.

The "lethal fantasy" of your story leaves little room for hope.

Of the nine stories in *The Encyclopedia of the Dead*, it is the only one in which death is not mitigated by the presence of the love whose fruit it is. Every type of love appears on the pages of the encyclopedia. "Red Stamps with Lenin's Picture" is a love story in the true sense of the word. Even "The Book of Kings and Fools" is tempered to some extent—or, to be more precise, set right —by a desperate gesture in the "Postscript."

1985

The Conscience of
an Unknown Europe

In Hourglass, *the final book in the triptych including* Early
Sorrows *and* Garden, Ashes, *you deal with the situation of
the Jews in Hungary during the Nazi period. Without pathos
—one of the striking features critics have noted about your work.
In a French magazine interview you state that despite the horror
of everything you as a writer might convey to the reader, what
you do in fact convey is an aesthetic impression. What really
matters is knowing how to start, carry on, and end a sentence.
But if that were so, literature would have nothing to do with the
emotions, would it?*

In the first place, you can't convey something that
doesn't exist; you can't bluff. A good reader—which according to Borges is rarer than a good writer—has no
trouble understanding or sensing that the person doing
the speaking, the author, has emotions. What you call
emotion—and what I might call rapture—is more often
present between the lines, between sentences, than in the
words themselves. I can't stress it enough: it's impossible,

absolutely impossible, to convey what doesn't exist. If you have no—what shall I call it?—inspiration, you won't inspire a soul, no matter how great your craft. But nothing must prevent writers from conveying what prompts them to write: the rapture, the . . . intense inspiration. In my case, form serves to keep feeling, emotion, from flowing too directly.

My second question may clarify my first. I'd like to hear what you have to say about a writer to whom emotion meant a great deal, a writer who wrote under the direct pressure of his political emotions: Louis-Ferdinand Céline. The only thing Céline cared about was emotion; to the consternation of the French journalists who interviewed him after the war, he declared that style is emotion. As you know, Céline was judged by many to be a villain, a fascist. Do you, who attribute such importance to form, think of Céline as a writer or a reactionary ideologue?

Céline has never made much of an impression on me. I don't know him well, and I'd rather not talk about him, actually. What I can say is that I have adopted a certain rigorous stance: I prefer making my emotions felt to expressing them outright. Céline, judging from the little I've read of him, is too direct. I don't care for emotional outpourings. I've started him, but he doesn't catch my interest: he's too . . . noisy for me, too eager to display his feelings. As I say, I prefer sentiments expressed between the lines and sentences.

Hourglass *ends on the following note: "It is better to be among the persecuted than among the persecutors." Céline, who took the part of the aggressors, must have thought the opposite. Yet he, too, became the butt of hatred and persecution. What good can come of being persecuted?*

The sentence you quote comes from the Talmud and belongs to a character of mine, so I'm under no obligation to defend it as my own. Still, I do tend to favor the position of martyrdom in principle: it strikes me as more honest from an absolute, moral point of view, to say nothing of the possible concrete ramifications. The ethical position of the persecuted is more acceptable than that of the persecutor.

Are there any political overtones to what you've just said?

No, no. It's got nothing to do with politics; it's a matter of absolute morality.

Fine, but mightn't the position of the persecuted afford a literary advantage? What I mean is, isn't it the persecuted of this world who produce literature?

Well put. Your question is my answer. I believe, as you say, that literature feeds on persecution and misfortune. One theory has it that literature is a kind of cure or at least the germ of a cure for the . . . evils of the world.

In Hourglass *you liken the Jew to a potato. You say the potato was introduced into Europe in the fourteenth century via Spain and is round and imperfect. Can you expand on the imperfections?*

Once more, it's a literary game. It comes from a letter written by E.S., the father—my father, if you will. Certain things in the novel can be explained only on the basis of irony, sarcasm. As E.S. writes the letter—it is 1944, the year the Jews were to be exterminated in Hungary—he feels the end is near; he writes it conscious of his own end. His future and the future of the Jews are crystal-clear to him, and he looks upon himself and the world of the Jews in general as imperfect. The association between potatoes and imperfection comes from the fact that he is dependent on the charity of his relatives at the time and is obliged to beg potatoes from them.

Is the father in the other two novels of the triptych, Early Sorrows *and* Garden, Ashes, *the same E.S., your father?*

Yes, though in the other two novels, which follow a logical and chronological order, his name is Eduard Scham. I assumed that readers who had gone through them would be equipped to recognize him. In addition, I wanted to give them the pleasure of discovering something for themselves. It all comes out at the end, chiefly in E.S.'s letter, which concludes, "Your loving brother, Eduard."

I'd like to hear what you have to say about another French writer, one you may not be so . . . indifferent to as you are to Céline. I'm referring to Proust. Like you, Proust was half-Jewish, but it was not an issue with him. A literary issue, I mean. Everyone knows that Proust stood up for Dreyfus in his private life, but in his novels the Dreyfus affair is merely a pretext for revolt in the bourgeois salons of the Third Republic. Then, too, he ridicules Bloch the Jew and Swann's "prophetic" outlook. Doesn't this make Proust a kind of reactionary, as people claimed at the time?

All that is history; it's not politics at all (though for some time now the history of French literature has been extremely politicized). You see, in my works being Jewish is a matter of chance, of destiny. Living as a child in Hungary during the war, I was obsessed by sin because I was persecuted by the children around me. I lived in fear and trembling. That is my only biography, the only world I know. What makes it attractive to literature is the fact that it has vanished, retreated into time. That and nothing else.

I refuse to be categorized as a Jewish writer. I am opposed to every variety of minority literature: feminist, homosexual, Jewish, black. I am equally opposed to any tightly defined concept of national literature. I think of literature as my country of origin. I am for Goethe's concept of world literature. I maintain that the Jewish problem in my work is not an intellectual issue; it is the only content of my life that can be called literary. It gives me everything I need: victim, executioner, distance in time. Because East European Jewry is no more. (Jews in Eastern Europe today live completely different lives.) It is a story of almost fantastic realism, dealing as it does with real things that no longer exist and are therefore enveloped in a kind of unreal mist, yet maintain their reality. Does that answer your question?

Yes, perfectly. But let me ask you one more thing about your relation to Judaism. Proust was Jewish on his mother's side, you on your father's side. Do you feel there is any fundamental difference? Is one more of a Jew when one's mother is Jewish, as Jewish law holds?

That is a matter of philosophy, religion, and ethnography. The only thing that mattered at the time was that most if not all my suffering came from my Jewish background. A child faced with the devastating reality of war couldn't possibly have thought of being Jewish as a scholastic problem. I had no idea why such awful things were happening to me, and people told me it was because I was Jewish. So I experienced it as a kind of punishment, especially since the catechism I had at school prepared me to accept the idea of guilt, Original Sin. In my novels I treat the issues less pointedly; I portray my environment and my father's environment from the perspective of a person asking himself questions, describing a situation that raises, that is bound to raise more questions than it can answer. That's the whole point.

Were you brought up a Catholic, then?
In school, yes. But at home I was brought up Orthodox. My mother was Orthodox; that is, a member of the Eastern Orthodox branch of Christianity. My religious education was a mix of things; Judaism was actually the smallest part of it.

I don't want to confuse what you think with what you write—as you say, literature plays on such things—but the character E.S., your father, is profoundly Jewish. Didn't that have an effect on you?
Like most Jews in that part of the world, especially Hungarian Jews, my father was an "unauthentic Jew," a Jew only insofar as others saw him as such, by the will of others, as Sartre put it. They were regarded as Jews, however, and therefore unable to integrate. E.S., not to say my father, did not really become a Jew until forced to, until made to wear the Star of David.

One trend in French literary theory traces the idea of modernity in literature back to Mallarmé and defines it as the destruction of the classical monologue or a "coup de dés," a toss of the dice. You wanted to be "modern" when you started writing at the age of twenty-five. What did modernity mean to you then? Does the issue still interest you? How do you define being modern?

Let me begin by saying I still want to be modern. But I don't mean that because things are constantly changing we need to keep up with them; I mean that there is something in the way a work is written and the times in which it is written that makes it a part of its age, that allows it to lay claim—as I do—to being "realistic." To be more specific, one of my major preoccupations—it runs through all my works—is to avoid misusing psychology, which the *nouveau roman* has shown (though more in theory than in practice) to be a thing of the past. Confronting imaginary characters with psychology is to my mind anachronistic, old hat, and the way I get away from it is by centering my novels on documents and documentation and convincing the reader—the good reader, the genuine reader, as Borges and Nabokov say—that what I write is based on reality and not pure invention. I've therefore used documents, records—some authentic, some not—from the first to the last of my novels.

Does this tenuous distinction between fiction and reality, truth and falsehood, correspond to the fantastic in literature?

I don't care for the word *fantastic*; in fact, I don't care for fantastic literature. The truth of the matter is, I'm a student of Russian literature, Russian realism. As Dostoevsky (whom I don't particularly care for either, by the way) once said: Nothing is more fantastic than reality. Granted, one of the stories in *The Encyclopedia of the Dead* has something of the fantastic in it. It's called "The Mirror of the Unknown." But even there I bring in documents to assure the reader of the truth of my fantasy. Sometimes, as I say, they're authentic, sometimes not. In the case of "The Mirror of the Unknown" I used a Hungarian newspaper and even mention it in the text.

A faits divers, *so to speak?*

Yes, news in brief. And because a newspaper contains the traces of history, I provide the reader with a kind of source.

Stalin's show trials, as you describe them in A Tomb for Boris Davidovich, *are unusual in the sense that they are entirely fictitious yet brutally true, the confessions being staged before a backdrop of death. Is Stalinism 'fantastic'?*

First, let me say a word about *A Tomb for Boris Davidovich.* I want to stress that the stories are based on absolutely authentic facts taken from books and documents. I wouldn't have dared invent such things, living in a country like Yugoslavia, because I'd have been accused—and rightly so—of anti-Communism. I needed proof, and my prime source was Karlo Štajner's *Seven Thousand Days in Siberia.* (I later wrote the preface to the French edition.) Obviously the documents are incomplete, because the reality of the concentration camps, especially before Solzhenitsyn, struck Western readers as unreal, not to say fantastic. In my case the process had to be reversed; that is, I had to find a fantastic way of writing realistically.

A Tomb for Boris Davidovich is a polemical work. It polemicized first and foremost with Master Borges and his *Universal History of Infamy*. I regarded Borges's title as exaggerated and still do, because the true history of infamy lies not in the petty murderers and brigands he described but in the camps. It also polemicized with Koestler's *Darkness at Noon*, which defends the position that forced confessions served the cause of the Party. Koestler argues that the people who confessed and the people who gave the orders worked in collusion, whereas we now know beyond a doubt that this was not so, that confessions were extorted by the cruelest, most barbarous methods.

Don't you think Koestler changed his mind before committing suicide?

I have no idea. Well informed and enlightened as he was, he could hardly have fathomed the reality of the situation at the time he wrote the novel. He was aware of the prisons and concentration camps, but unfamiliar with the methods used by the Soviets.

Suicide occurs quite often in your novels. There is Fräulein Weiss in Garden, Ashes, *who keeps trying to kill herself, who tries so often, as you put it, that she discovers her immortality! Eduard Scham, too, thinks seriously of committing suicide on several occasions. Attila József, a Hungarian poet you've translated, killed himself by placing his head on a railway track. What about writers' suicides? Is suicide a corollary of literature?*

Russian literature is a mine of suicides, but suicide is not particularly characteristic of writers. Personally, I'm more intrigued by the suicide of Marx's son-in-law Paul Lafargue—socialist, revolutionary, and philosopher—than by that of Attila József. Lafargue and his wife killed themselves at the age of seventy to preclude the decline in their physical and intellectual faculties. They killed themselves on their wedding anniversary, the result of a decision they had made when still young.

Suicide represents what I'd call a privileged moment in the life of an individual. Whereas—banal but true—we can't chose the moment we come into the world, choosing the moment to leave is an eminently human act. Like virtually everything in my work, here, too, the empirical takes precedence over the academic or literary: I've felt very close to people who have wished to kill themselves and settle a score with life. I think of Koestler's example as . . . as the crowning of a life. It's not something that just happens to a person at one time or another; it's a privilege.

Couldn't one contrast this type of behavior with another, which might be illustrated by the patience of a Borges?

Yes, Borges married at the very end of his life. A beautiful thing to do, a . . . metaphysical gesture—joining two cardinal points of life: marriage and death. Why, it's almost a Borges story. Looking back on it now, I don't feel Borges left this world with serene expectations. Marriage meant a kind of blood transfusion and, as I say, a metaphysical gesture: an attempt to forestall the coming of death through the presence of another. Yes, it was his last story.

All writers "converse" with their forerunners or contemporaries: Borges with the English and Cervantes, Proust with Saint-Simon, Céline with Proust. Who are your favorite conversation partners?

"Conversation partners"—I like that. Very French! Far better than "influences." Well, first I must name two relatively unknown Yugoslav writers: Andrić and Krleža; then two Russians: Babel and Pilnyak; one Frenchman: Rabelais. And of course Borges and Joyce.

Is it humor that links Rabelais, Borges, and Joyce?

No. What matters most to me is the way they embrace reality in literary form, the fact that they give reality an effective, the most effective possible, literary form.

The Encyclopedia of the Dead, *a collection of stories, is full of false clues, intentional confusion of fiction and reality, allusions to books and encyclopedias, wars and revolutions. All very Borgesian in theme, wouldn't you say?*

Hold on, now. What Borges did for modern literature is indisputable. But I was a Borgesian before I knew him. Let's say he reinforced the Borgesian tendency in me. By the way, you'll find a lot of Borges in the two Russian writers I've just mentioned. The sort of erudition having no goal other than to embrace reality with the greatest possible precision and incorporate the broadest reality in the narrowest confines. A hundred pages of a novel, for instance.

When did you come into contact with Borges's work?

In the seventies, when he first came out in Serbo-Croatian.

You share more with Borges than theme; you share style as well. The taut sentence structure of A Tomb for Boris Davidovich *is worthy of a Borges.*

Borges once said that a book with no counterbook does not deserve to exist. *A Tomb for Boris Davidovich* is the counterbook to *A Universal History of Infamy*. It is both homage and polemic. But what I really have from Borges is the lyrical element of the *poète manqué*. Lyricism is dangerous in prose, and if I constantly purge my texts, cut them, if I'm sarcastic, it's to keep lyricism from gaining the upper hand.

True, you're more interested in finding form for content than in academic classification, but in Hourglass *the question-and-answer format gives the narrative a dialogic structure, in* Early Sorrows *you come close to the genre of Jules Renard's classic novel of childhood* Poil de Carotte, *in* Garden, Ashes *you are quite Proustian, and in* A Tomb for Boris Davidovich *and* The Encyclopedia of the Dead *you are Borgesian. By changing so much, don't you end with no style at all?*

Oh no. There's my sensibility and then certain "tics" that turn up in all my works. The mixture of irony and lyricism, for instance. Besides, I feel that every subject requires a different form, a different approach, a state of mind corresponding more or less to an ideal style. You might say I feel the need for a change in tempo. After a while the old rhythm no longer appeals to me; I need to move on to something else.

Well, you're certainly at your most Proustian in Garden, Ashes. *The young man who tells the story has all the symptoms of the Proustian narrator: the panic fear of falling asleep before his mother kisses him, the compulsive need for his mother's presence, the nerves, the obsessions . . . What exactly is your debt to Proust?*

Proust doesn't leave me cold, that's for certain, but he's not an author who makes you want to . . . follow suit. *Garden, Ashes* may well bear traces of his mythology of childhood, except that I look at things from a different angle. The chronology is different. *Garden, Ashes* isn't the first book in the trilogy; it begins with *Early Sorrows*, proceeds with *Garden, Ashes*—which, in addition to the boy, introduces the father, my father, or the character Eduard Scham—and ends with *Hourglass*, in which E.S. predominates.

And in Proust the father character is completely neglected.

Right. But what is more important, I needed three distinct approaches to re-create my expanding world. In France the last two volumes of the trilogy appeared before the first. The wrong way round. To preserve the continuity, I asked (well, demanded) that Gallimard publish it in a different series. It appeared as a children's book, though, as the subtitle makes clear, that's not strictly speaking what it is. To use a line from Max Jacob, it's a book for children and other sensitive readers.

Since Flaubert there's been a conception of style as ineluctable revision, obsessive return to a given manner of writing. Flaubert never stopped cutting, Proust never stopped adding, and Céline merely inserted exclamation marks. Do you see an analogous stylistic recurrence in your works? Are you obsessive?

Of the writers you mention I am closest to Flaubert: I condense too much. Hence the brevity of my novels. I take writing very seriously, so much so that I write only when I can't help writing. But let's not go into detail

about that. Motivation is always existential: I write because I call my whole life into question.

Writing is therapy, though belated therapy, therapy as
an afterthought, because as long as the depression lasts the
cure won't work. (I mean an illness, not a mania.) When
I write I'm in indirect yet intimate contact with the subject that I've chosen—or that's chosen me. Writing is my
way of finding release from obsessions, and the device that
triggers the consolation mechanism is suffering. All the
rest is secondary and . . . technical.

Yes, I cut. That's the technical side of things, if you
will, the side that gets transmitted to the typewriter. The
typewriter functions for me as protection from the invasion of feelings, from the trembling of the hand, meta-
phorically speaking. A sentence typed out on a machine
is as neutral as a sentence thought up by a stranger: it can
be corrected or erased as if it came from a hack. From
time to time I find a sentence that pleases me. Correction
by self-destruction, you might call it. And because I have
a mania for reading the same passages a hundred times, I
get more and more bored with my own manuscript. You
might say that what's left after the long repetitions is what
has managed to hold out against my boredom mechanism!

*One more question about style. Sainte-Beuve, the nineteenth-
century French critic, made a practice of studying writers' lives so
as to reconstruct what he called "the botany of the mind." The
psychological school of criticism he founded drew an intimate connection between creativity and a writer's work habits, weaknesses,
vices, "foibles." Have you any foibles?*

I am lazy. To be truthful, I seldom work, and when I
do, I live for months in prodigious, frightful disorder, a

physical disorder extending to the objects around me. Work is a sort of struggle to coax something pure and definitive out of that disorder. I write in disorder to create clarity, to inject the order of my sentences and spirit into the disorder of my thoughts and objects.

Some French critics and theoreticians believe the novel as a genre is on the way out, that it's in retreat from the fragmentary nature of the contemporary world. The Cuban writer Cabrera Infante refuses to be called a novelist; Borges never wrote a novel. In Brazil, good contemporary writers like Ruben Fonseca and Raduan Nassar are known for their stories or novellas. What about you? Do you think of yourself as a novelist?

Cabrera Infante? What has he written? Oh, I remember. *Three Trapped Tigers*. No, I didn't like it, I couldn't finish it. Those theories—they're mostly French, and the French think their own problems are universal. But look at the American novel: it's doing fine. The Central European novel, too. And the Latin American novel. I personally don't believe the novel is on its way out; I believe it's being transformed into the commercial novel, something that both partakes of the literary heritage—the psychological novel, the realistic novel, and so on—and distorts it. That's what is so alarming. A good novel no longer has an audience. It's like good music: it's being replaced by "pop." The fact is, we're witnessing a "de-novelization" of taste, and literature is becoming a rarity. You can't deny it: the bestseller is the genre of the century. No, the novel isn't on its way out; it's multiplying, even becoming a kind of cancer, but there's no crisis.

As for me, I wouldn't call myself a novelist, but that's because of the structure (much as I hate the word) of what

I write. If we could find some other name for the genre. Unamuno liked to call it a *nimen* instead of a *roman*. His little joke.

Has there been a degeneration at least?

Never have more novels been written. I'm talking only about quantity, of course, not quality. Still, it's a good trend. It establishes a distance between the general public and the elite, the sort of elite audience that existed before romanticism.

Would you agree that your way of looking at things is hardly progressive?

I'm opposed to populism, opposed to flirtation on the part of the writer with the average reader. The mind must regain what distinguishes it from mediocrity, its aura.

Hasn't this sort of attitude caused problems for you in Yugoslavia? Aren't you persona non grata there?

Misunderstandings rather than problems, and no, I visit Yugoslavia two or three times a year. If I get on people's nerves there, it's more for my books than for my attitudes, though they, too, stem from my stand on literature. In any case, I write for the cultivated reader. I believe the category exists; I know it does: it's my audience.

Are you read more in France than in Yugoslavia?

No, my widest audience is in Yugoslavia, but I have a worldwide readership—limited but real—and the reader of my works is familiar with the Bible, Homer, Ovid, Dante, Rabelais, Tolstoy, etc. Such readers do exist. I might add that I have received a number of literary prizes in Yugoslavia. In 1984 *The Encyclopedia of the Dead* was awarded the prize that bears the name of our Nobel laureate Ivo Andrić.

Why did you leave Yugoslavia? Isn't Paris a sort of exile?
Let me put it laconically: it's a Joyce-like exile, a self-imposed exile.

When did you settle in France?
Let me see. In about 1980.

Are there any good writers in France today?
I sincerely respect the integrity of the two Marguerites: Duras and Yourcenar. Though I'm not, in fact, a great novel reader.

You've translated poets from the Russian (Esenin), the Hungarian (Attila József), and the French (Lautréamont, Baudelaire, Verlaine, Prévert, Queneau). Are you a poet?
I've never published my poems, thank God, though, oddly enough, I've spent my whole life preparing to be a poet. In the end I find that the things I have to say, the things I'm obsessed by, I can say better in prose. Translation is consolation, a way of making a poem I really love my own. That's why I keep doing it. Though it may also be a form of cynicism.

Does translating mean translating form?
Our tradition—which was once the French tradition, but is no longer—is to translate a sonnet as a sonnet, an alexandrine as an alexandrine, a rhyme as a rhyme. Some of our translators have tried to introduce the *méthode ap-*

proximative currently used in France, but it doesn't work. Mallarmé represents the high point of this French deviation: he was perfectly capable of writing sugary poems for the ladies, but when he translated a poem he translated it into prose. It may be a Cartesian tendency.

What's your opinion of reviewers? Barthes felt they always arrived at the wrong time: when a book was out and had ceased to be of interest to its author, when it was a dead letter.

Strange to say, though, I'm interviewed more often in France than in Yugoslavia. I've noticed that it is the Yugoslav reviewers who write only what I say in interviews: their reviews are pure repetition. When *The Encyclopedia of the Dead* came out, I decided to let them go it on their own. The results were disastrous.

What about the French reviewers?

I have no faith in reviewers on principle. Nothing external to a book—TV, the press, any branch of the media—can affect its life, its survival. But I do think that the media are responsible for the democratization—the destruction—of aesthetic taste.

One last question: The little boy in Garden, Ashes *is so frightened of dying he can't sleep, and tries to come up with a plan that will free him from death. Can we say that your oeuvre is the plan and you are the character?*

Works or books rather than oeuvre—that's another word I don't like. But no, I don't think so. I got over academic notions such as eternal glory or immortality through literature when I was sixteen. With death the work disappears in spirit. Immortality based on a body of literature is a rhetorical figure in the French manner, don't you agree? Early on, I switched to Heine's line, which runs something like: "I prefer the embrace of a pretty reader to glory after death." Though when I cross the Styx on Charon's ferry I may want to have my complete works with me. I might find it easier to die.

1986

Life, Literature

I'd like to devote the first part of our interview to biographical facts that may be of interest to your readers. Despite your known resistance to biographical data and the biographical approach to your work, I believe that much of it—especially the novels you have called the "autobiographical triptych" (Early Sorrows; Garden, Ashes; Hourglass)*—shows your childhood to have been of fundamental importance to your literary development. So let's try to delineate the part played by autobiographical material in your work on the one hand and imagination and illusion on the other.*

My whole childhood is an illusion, an illusion that has fed my imagination, and after writing two or three books on the theme of "early sorrows," I feel that degrading the imagination to "biographical facts" is rank reductionism. Life cannot be reduced to books, but neither can books be reduced to life. After I related the events of my childhood in a lyrical, consistent, definitive form, that form became an integral part of my childhood, my only childhood. Even I have trouble now distinguishing between the two illusions: living truth and literary truth; they are so intertwined that it is next to impossible to trace a dividing line between them, and any other interpretation, especially by the author, is likely to impoverish them. Paraphrasing a poem diminishes its spirit, its rhythm, its élan, and reduces its metaphors to a common language. Somewhere Gérard Genette quotes La Fontaine's line *"Sur les ailes du temps, la tristesse s'envole"* (Sadness takes flight on the wings of time) in a rhetorian's "translation" as *"Le chagrin ne dure pas toujours"* (No sorrow lasts forever).

I understand your fears, but I can't help thinking, literature aside, that the facts of your childhood are not devoid of interest.

Every biography, especially of a writer, involves a certain reductionism unless it has had the fortune to have been given artistic form: it is the unique and inimitable story of a unique and inimitable person in a unique and inimitable time. The ideal biography would encompass all people in all times, and the only way of providing such an illusion, especially when the subject is childhood, is through "poetic," literary form.

Isn't there a paradox in what you say? On the one hand, you try to show the living truth in your work; on the other hand, you treat it—the specific source feeding the work—as private and thus unliterary, irrelevant.

Literature uses the specific, of course, to get at the general, but without literary transposition every specific, biographical detail, everything that sets you apart from others, everything that's private to the nth degree, the distinguishing features on your identity card, seems like a facial growth or a physical defect. Literature feeds on the specific, the individual, and is at pains to integrate it—short of losing track of it—into the general. That's why I so oppose reducing a work of literature to a life and object to literary biography that overemphasizes the particular and fails to integrate the subject's "distinguishing features" into human destiny as a whole; that's why I reject all "minority" literature and literary ghettos. When feminism, homosexualism, or Judaism takes over, it turns into a form of reductionism. And ideological reductionism is the worst of all.

We'll have more to say about that later. For the present, let's go back to your childhood. You stress its importance for your development and speak of it as a theme that enables you to integrate the general and the specific most readily.

Childhood is the time of life when we have the strongest common denominator regardless of race, surroundings, or historical period, when we come closest to the hypothetical biography of all people at all times. Later the common denominator begins to fade, differences make themselves felt, and the specific gains ground over the general.

But despite the common denominator of childhood you can't deny that in your case times and origins were major contributing factors to the "difference" that so marks your writing. That's why I keep coming back to biography—or, if you will, fate.

The points you make are crucial. If not for the ambiguity of my origins, if not for the "troubling strangeness" created by my being Jewish, if not for the hardships of a wartime childhood, I'd never have become a writer.

Then let's begin at the beginning. Your dust jackets tell us you were born in Subotica "on the border between Yugoslavia and Hungary." What did and does the town of Subotica mean to you?

I presume that the reason my parents chose the Subotica maternity hospital was that they were friendly with a doctor there. A Jew, probably. But the real significance of the town—called Subotica in Serb and Szabadka in Hungarian and situated "on the border between Yugoslavia and Hungary"—is that it represents a duality, an ambiguity of language, origin, history, and culture, thus testifying to the fact that nothing in a writer's life is accidental, not even the accident of birthplace.

Am I to take it that you have no memory of the town where you were born?

My first sensory impressions of childhood go back to Novi Sad, which is located a hundred or so kilometers south of Subotica, on the Danube. Smells, tastes, colors. The smell of chestnut blossoms, of roses in a vase, of camomile, machine oil in the sewing machine, my father's cigarettes, cologne on my mother's neck, clean sheets, urine, the oilcloth on the table, coffee, soap, spices, the leather sweat band on my father's hat, cab seats, railway stations, pharmacies, an empty first-class compartment, the strap that opens the compartment window, a leather suitcase. The taste of cod-liver oil, of honey, of café au lait, of cinnamon, wooden crayons, paste, ink, paper, rubber, candy, blood from my finger, tincture of iodine, tears, cough medicine. Colors: the dark green on one side of chestnut leaves and the light green on the other, the fireworks of the kaleidoscope, the hues of the rainbow in glass marbles, the rust of autumnal decay, the azure of the sky, the white of the clouds, the dirty yellow of the house fronts. And images (it's like leafing through old postcards): the artesian well on the corner, the straw that covered it in winter, a row of chestnut trees with rustling leaves auguring stormy weather, single-story houses opening on courtyards, low windows decked out with bright red and pale pink geraniums and dusty lawns in front, squeaky delivery carts and cabs floating down the street like gondolas, the courtyards of the poor; bluing dissolving in the tin trough outside the laundry, the foul-smelling drain hole waiting for slops, the barracks and the cemetery, the cathedral and the synagogue, the Orthodox Church of the Assumption, where I was baptized at the age of four (the priest pouring water over my head as I look all over for my mother—who has entrusted me for the moment to my godfather—the smell of incense, the chant of the priest, the flicker of the candles, the faces of the saints on the icons), the trams with their lyre-like pantographs, the photographer's studio with artificial flowers and a real bird in a cage, the lace on the velvet seats in first-class compartments, my mother's cathedral-shaped Singer sewing machine . . .

Your images have quite an idyllic, peacetime quality to them.

But the photo-album idyll they represent came to an abrupt end when I was torn from my sleep one night by a volley of shots fired under our window. My mother turned on a light, but turned it off immediately and took me out of bed in the dark. I knew I wasn't dreaming or having a nightmare: my mother was trembling. The lamp going on and off and the pitch black under the bed in the dark room—that was the end of the luminous, sunny scenes crowding my memories until then. Suddenly everything was opaque or murky like a roll of film exposed in a darkroom.

What year was that?

1942, January, the start of the tragic "cold days," which is a euphemistic metaphor for the barbaric massacre of the Jews and Serbs of the Vojvodina. If I'd been able to make connections between certain events and changes, I mightn't have been taken unawares. There were certain indications—our frequent changes of address, for example. By moving from one street to another—from a better place to a worse one—my father was following the logic of his financial ruin, but, more important, he was hoping that with a little luck he might pass for Aryan. If on the first day of the "raid" we had an arrow cross (the symbol of the Hungarian fascists) daubed on our door at 21 Bem (formerly German) Street and not a yellow star (which was painted on houses where Jews were living), it was not just because our landlady was Hungarian but also because my father had managed to conceal his true identity from her. How disappointed she must have been a week later when she saw a Star of David on his chest. But I didn't grasp all this until long after the fact, when I could put it into a historical framework. At the time I was completely cut off from time and space: I had no idea what day, what year, what century it was. I was like a trembling puppy. That is why I prefer to speak in images.

Did you wear a star, too?

No, but since the son of a mixed marriage was regarded by law as belonging to the father's religion and the daughter to the mother's, my mother made two Stars of David on her sewing machine—one large, the other small—from remnants of the silk used for quilts. My father and I stood in front of her, as stiff as if at the tailor's, while she, pins in mouth, slid the stars up and down our coat lapels. Was my father brave enough to flout the authorities in my case, or did my certificate of baptism provide him with a loophole? I don't know. The yellow star looked like a dandelion. It spent ages in the drawer of my mother's sewing machine amid thread of all colors, snippets of cloth, and buttons, but after the "dress rehearsal" that day I never wore it.

To the best of my knowledge, the yellow-star episode appears in none of your stories or novels. Why?

You're right. I've never put it in any of my writings. It seemed too strong, too charged, like many other episodes I've been unable to neutralize with an ironic counterweight. There's something shameful about suffering.

You were seven at the time. What impression did the "cold days" make on you? How much do you remember?

There is no continuity in what I remember, only disjointed images, fuzzy views of a winter landscape and gray dawn. Through the blackened windows I could hear shouts, the crunch of steps in the frozen snow, and occasional snow-muffled shots like tears smothered under a feather pillow. My father gave my sister and me a Hungarian magazine and told us to hold it up high so the title was clearly visible. The magazine featured pictures from the Eastern front—a Hungarian soldier being welcomed by Ukrainian peasants with icons and bread and salt, a girl with blond braids embracing a young tank driver, houses in flames, the brutal landscape of the Russian steppe. Holding a magazine in a language I didn't know struck me as a dangerous trick that could easily be exposed and land us in trouble.

What language did you speak at home?

My father, like most Jews in our part of the Dual Monarchy, was equally comfortable in Hungarian, German, and Serb. At home, though, we spoke only Serb, and in 1940 I started attending the Serb elementary school. In 1942 I waved the Yugoslav flag and shouted with my class, "*Bolje rat nego pakt!*" (Better war than the pact!)—a sentence memorable for its assonant rhyme but whose mysterious meaning went over my head—and every barbershop window had its portrait of young King Peter in three-quarter face, as on postage stamps.

When you described the shots under your window just now, you spoke of your mother, not your father, protecting you, and although you switched immediately to your father, he seems to have been a secondary figure.

That's probably because, as you've noticed, I think in images and am always groping in the dark. The scenes where my father appears are negatives in a sense, images of his absence. To this day I picture him climbing into cars, cabs, trains, or trams. We are either waiting for him or seeing him off. Or I see him during a short visit to Kovin (the local equivalent of Bedlam) in September

1939, asking my mother for scissors to cut short his suffering: it's late summer, autumn rust is starting to eat away at plane-tree leaves, and my father is sitting in his hospital pajamas on a wooden bench in the hospital grounds, an absent look in his eyes. Or before our last visit, in 1944, in the improvised ghetto in Zalaegerszeg, from which he never returned. That accounts for my need to reconstitute his image, fill in the void between two of his apparitions, discover him in the background of a family snapshot. It's rather like the way I construct characters for whom I have a few documentary details, a few inadequate facts I have to expand to fill the yawning gaps between them, and only the solid matter of the imagination, matter whose power of conviction has documentary force, will do.

Yet in your autobiographical triptych you devote much less space to your mother than to your father.

The father who appears in my works under the name of Eduard Scham, or E.S., is an idealized projection unencumbered by the solid, homogeneous mass of realities and memories. He is therefore a doubly negative character, negative by his absence and negative as a literary hero. He is an invalid, an alcoholic, a neurasthenic, and a Jew —in a word, ideal material for a literary character. As for the mother, I believe that in creating her character I was motivated more by literary than by psychological considerations. The fact that the mother is a positive hero kept me from treating her with the necessary salutary ironic detachment. Love, like beauty and suffering, is too charged with emotion. Let me remind you that in Tolstoy's *Childhood, Boyhood, Youth* the mother is pale and schematic in comparison with the father.

Was it simply to set up an intellectual balance between the two characters that you depicted the mother in the novel Garden, Ashes *as the person who opened up the world of the imagination and poetry?*

Here, too, I relied chiefly on memory, on facts. My mother knew a lot of poems, both epic and lyric, and a lot of fairy tales and legends, and filled the gaps in her memory (in a Hungarian backwater without a single Serb book) out of her imagination, sometimes sticking as close as possible to the original she had forgotten, sometimes improvising on the theme with major digressions. Some of her poetic flights were too clearly applicable to our life and situation for me to believe them faithful to the original, though I may have misjudged things. In this first encounter with poetry I may simply have discovered—though on the basis of a false assumption—its very essence; namely, that poetry is always about the person reading or hearing it.

Do you know what your mother read?

When she was young, she read novels and verse with a naïve enthusiasm that makes no distinction between literature and life. She sighed over the poems of Njegoš, the Montenegrin prince and poet of Nicholas I, and over his verse translation of Chateaubriand's *The Last of the Abencérages.* The Oriental splendor of Moorish and Spanish palaces left a clear trace on her literary sensibility, which—like that of all amateurs—tended toward the romantic.

You once said in this connection that the figure of the mother in Garden, Ashes *was distorted by the English translation. What did you mean?*

The case is instructive in several ways but primarily with respect to translation. Translating literature takes more than a knowledge of two languages; it takes a knowledge of two cultures, two civilizations. The English translation (and the Hebrew one, which was made from it) introduces Homer and Mérimée into one of the chapters featuring the mother: the translator, misled by the vagaries of transliteration, transformed Omer and Merima, the heroes of a Muslim ballad very popular in our country, into Homer and Mérimée! This upset the balance between the characters of the father and the mother. While the father in the novel—as you've pointed out—is a man of learning, the mother is his foil: erudition versus spontaneity; the Bible and the Talmud (because the Timetable is a Talmudic book, a commentary) versus folk (oral) poetry.

What is the ballad about?
    The love of a Pyramus and Thisbe, or a Romeo and Juliet:

> *Two young people fell in love,*
> *A boy named Omer, a girl named Merima.*

Though our traditional decasyllabic line gives a Homeric ring to it, don't you think? So the mistake isn't that terrible, after all. You might even say the good spirit Euterpe, who watches over manuscripts and protects them from all evils, made certain it healed the way a wound heals. If you remember, Mérimée was responsible for the hoax known as *La Guzla*, a work that appeared in France during the 1830s, purporting to be "Illyrian folk poetry," which brought our folk poetry to the attention of the world (fooling even Pushkin, who, convinced the poems were of Serb origin, translated them into Russian). Thus, the spirit of Omer and Merima inspired Mérimée's imaginary folk poet Hyacinth Maglanovič and in the English translation of my novel Homer and Mérimée are simply metonymic figures for folk poetry. My mother may well have read them.

Were your mother's lyrical flights an attempt to awaken a love of literature in you? Did she perhaps sense you had a gift for literature?

Living in Hungary, a foreign country whose language she never fully mastered, my mother recited poems and told stories primarily as a means of appeasing her own terrible loneliness, but also, I think, to maintain something of her tradition in her son: she was afraid that if my native language became alien to me she might become alien to me.

Who was your mother? Who were your maternal ancestors?

My maternal ancestors were warriors. Actually, everybody was a warrior in Montenegro, and an enormous revolver worn in the belt without a holster was as integral a part of a man's dress as his cap. And although Montenegrin genealogy is not matrilinear—which makes it basically different from Jewish family law—a great-grandmother on my mother's side is still remembered in family legend as an Amazon who chopped off the head of a Turkish tyrant. My grandfather fought in many battles, then broke the long epic tradition in about 1910 by going to work for the post office, supervising the installation of telegraph lines across the wilds of Montenegro.

My mother was related to a *vojvoda* or governor by the name of Marko Miljanov whose ethnographic works—especially *Examples of Honor and Heroism*—are still of interest as both ethnographic and literary texts. Miljanov was a famous warrior who was illiterate until the age of fifty. His handwriting was square and firm, and because he used neither paragraphs nor punctuation his manuscripts look like clay tablets. One of my uncles, Risto Dragićević, studied in Belgrade and at the Jagellonian University in Warsaw. His writings on the history of Montenegro and his studies of the poet-prince Njegoš are considered authoritative. His library, which was especially rich in dictionaries and encyclopedias, was a source of Baudelairean dreams during my Cetinje school days: *Le Petit Larousse illustré*, 1923 edition, with its prints and color plates and its motto *"Je sème à tout vent,"* planted the seed of a dangerous curiosity in me.

Yet in the end your family triptych seems more the quest for a father. Who was your father? Who were his ancestors?

Judging from the surname Kohn (Kohen, Cohen, from which the title of the Khazar kings, *kogan*, appears to derive), one of my great-grandfathers was a rabbi. Certain references in my father's letters suggest that his forebears were feather merchants and came to Hungary after being expelled from Alsace. I imagine he was referring to ancestors on his mother's side. The frequent malicious allusions to feather merchants, meant to remind his wealthy nieces of their humble origins, were a Talmudic lesson of sorts, an admonition. My father's father was a merchant and landowner. The wood in the forests he owned was burned to make potash, a substance used in the manufacture of tile stoves and cooking ware. Whether he was ruined by a fire or by competition from Bohemian porcelain, which greatly reduced the demand for potash, I don't know. By the time I started taking an interest in where the family came from, who we were, where we were going, the documents were lost and the keepers of family lore gone, dead in the Holocaust.

My father was born in western Hungary, which at the time belonged to the Dual Monarchy. Probably with a view to assimilation, he Hungarianized his name when he was thirteen. He went to the Trade Academy at Zalaegerszeg, the birthplace of a certain Mr. Virág, who, thanks to a certain Mr. Joyce, achieved notoriety under the name of Bloom, Leopold Bloom. After several unsuccessful business ventures, my father found employment in the Ministry of Railways, where he eventually reached the rank of chief inspector. As a result, until 1942 we traveled free of charge in first-class compartments, and the guards saluted him as if he were a general. His *Bus, Ship, Rail, and Air Travel Guide* later became famous thanks to my novels.

We obviously can't keep to a strict chronological order, but let's go back to Novi Sad and January 1942. What happened on that day?

We're fast-forwarding a little, I see. Well, my sister and I are sitting on the sofa, leaning on each other and holding a Hungarian magazine, "so people can see the title." On one page there's a picture of a tank in the snow. It's been hit by a shell and looks like a man punched in the solar plexus. There are soldiers with their hands up standing next to it and other soldiers aiming guns at them. In a montage that almost anticipates an early literary device of mine, two realities come together: two soldiers and a policeman burst into the house, bayonets gleaming; one soldier looks under the bed and opens the cupboards; the other holds his rifle at the ready; my father shows the policeman his papers; the policeman returns them; they leave. Take One.

Take Two. An hour later the action is repeated down to the last sequence: after my father shows the policeman his papers and the policeman returns them, my father takes his hat and coat from the clothes rack; he wonders whether to take his cane; the abandoned cane swings back and forth on the clothes rack.

I presume you use the cinematic approach because it enables you to register images and experiences with the greatest possible distance.

Right. It provides a certain defamiliarization, *ostranenie* as Shklovsky put it; it breaks down "automatic perception."

Do you apply it primarily to personal experience?

Not exclusively.

Let's go back to the "cold days." What happened to you? Where did they take your father?

My role as a witness ends with the scene I've just described. What follows is a reconstruction based on documents and scraps of survivors' memories.

We pan along the frozen Danube, stopping at a hole hacked in the glassy ice near the wooden changing cabins of the town beach. We see a board stretching across the hole, then soldiers milling about. Frost coats their mustaches; steam pours from their nostrils. Suddenly a young woman emerges from the direction of the cabins, naked. She is holding a girl by the hand. The girl is naked, too. Their skin is reddish-blue with the cold. The soldiers push them onto the board. They shoot them in the head or stab them with their bayonets. The victims fall into the dark green water. A civilian shoves them under the ice with a boat hook. The scene is shot from the divine perspective of a gray, wintry cloud that voices cannot reach. Unflinching, the camera recedes to reveal long lines of people beyond the cabins. It is now so high that we cannot make out faces; we can scarcely distinguish men, women, and children.

Yet somewhere at the end of the line, among the latest truckloads, we single out a man in a hat, glasses, and threadbare gray coat, and if we can see no one else it is because whoever positioned the camera up there (to avoid the trap of detail, nudity, and humiliation, when the body reacts instinctively to the fear of death; to avoid scenes of rape, smashed skulls, and blood on the trampled snow; to avoid voices, screams, howls, pleas, prayers, and supplications; in other words, to achieve divine objectivity in this world without God) is too biased to keep from zooming in on his father.

In an earlier interview you said your father was "saved by a miracle," and the miracle was that the hole in the ice was plugged up by corpses.

A technical glitch that meant no more than a stay of execution. Still, international opinion apparently got wind of the Hungarian military's barbarous behavior and someone intervened and put at least a temporary halt to the massacre. My father came home late that afternoon, broken, suddenly aged, and with the terrifying look he'd had in Kovin three years earlier. The day he spent on the Danube, waiting his turn by the cabins, the anteroom of hell (he couldn't help hearing the shots, the screams, the splashing), completely ruined his already shaken health.

What form did his illness take?

He had occasional attacks of anxiety neurosis, a diagnosis I didn't learn about until thirty years after his death. So it was only in retrospect, many years after the fact, that I came to understand what I'd observed during our 1939 visit to Kovin. Even though I wasn't quite five at the time, I have an exceptionally clear memory of the ride in the cab, the hospital grounds, the striped pajamas, just as I remember the scene I told you about a moment ago, when he asked my mother to leave him a pair of scissors on the pretext that he needed them to cut the knot in a rubber band.

How did you find out about the diagnosis?

In the seventies I wrote a television play called *Night and Fog*. It came to me after a visit to Hungary, a pilgrimage to the places where we had lived during the war. After the play was shown on Belgrade television, I received a letter from a Mrs. G. in Novi Sad telling me she had recognized my father in the person whose past the hero of my play was searching for. Since I was working on *Hourglass* at the time, I looked upon any information about my father as a godsend. He was like a historical figure whose life was little known. When she realized I knew something about his mental condition and even that he had spent some time in Kovin, Mrs. G. told me in her formal, imperial-royal manner (we were speaking Hungarian), "Your dear father told me and my late husband that as part of his treatment he wrote the story of his life for the doctor." Which for me was the equivalent of Columbus's diary or the notes of Didacus Spirus! The next day I went to Kovin with a psychiatrist friend, Dr. Smodlak, and told them my father had been treated there in 1939 for delirium tremens. The hospital director's young assistant came back with a file that was obviously my father's—the name and birthplace were right—but the diagnosis was anxiety neurosis, not delirium tremens. He also told me that my father had spent three months there in 1934. But the rest of his records had been lost during the war, and there was no biography in the patient's hand.

Did the new diagnosis give you a different picture of your father as hero of your novel?

It was a revelation. After reading up on psychopathology and anxiety neurosis, I started seeing all kinds of things more clearly. I learned first that anxiety neurosis had long been thought an endemic condition of the Jewish intelligentsia of Central Europe; second, that patients often took to drink to drown their latent fears; and third, that the disorder was congenital in ten to twenty percent of the cases according to some scholars and in seventy to ninety percent according to others. At last I was able to account for the traumatic fears that had plagued me on two or three occasions in my youth but that fortunately lasted for only a few days.

Can you describe them?

It's not easy. The suffering was hideous. A kind of "metaphysical fear," fear and trembling. All of a sudden, with no visible exterior cause, the defense mechanism that lets you live with the knowledge of human mortality goes to pieces, and a menacing lucidity comes over you—an absolute lucidity, I'd call it. I've described it—that condition of an intense inner trembling—in a chapter of *Hourglass.*

I believe you're referring to one of the sections of "Notes of a Madman" which makes a connection between the hero's psychological crisis and the Danube massacre. You've also given a description of the "cold days" in your novel Psalm 44.

I wrote *Psalm 44*—a novella, actually—in less than a month when I was twenty-five for a competition sponsored by the Jewish Association in Belgrade. The jury members, which included the surrealist poet and novelist Ljubiša Jocić, were convinced it had been written by a woman: they found it full of both "feminine psychology" and "feminine sensibility." I based it on a brief newspaper item (it dealt with the visit made by a couple and their child to the camp where the child was born to them in the last days of the war), which enabled me to treat the rather unusual plot as reality. The weakness of that piece of juvenilia is not so much the plot—though it is too charged, overwrought—as the fatal absence of ironic detachment, an element that later became an integral part of my literary approach.

You've told me you didn't want to publish it.

I was more or less aware of its weaknesses at the time,

but when I offered the publishers my first novel, *The Attic*, they said it was too short, and since they knew I had won first prize in a literary contest they insisted on publishing the two short novels together.

Yet you reissued Psalm 44 *as a separate work in the recent edition of your complete works.*

Yes, because I realized that, in the framework of everything I'd written, it had a definite function: it showed me searching and coming of age. At the same time, those first two short novels, *The Attic* and *Psalm 44*, though different in theme, composition, and style, exemplify the parallel lines I'd follow in all subsequent works: metaphysical obsession on the one hand and historical, "documentary" reconstruction on the other. Not that these themes or preoccupations are entirely separable: in my later works they're often interwoven. But you can still follow the parallel threads. There is a clear stylistic similarity between *Psalm 44*, which deals with German camps, and *A Tomb for Boris Davidovich*, written some fifteen years later about Soviet camps, just as there is a certain unity of style between *The Attic* and, say, *Garden, Ashes*, especially in the interpenetration of lyrical impulse and ironic detachment. *Hourglass* and *The Encyclopedia of the Dead* might be seen as syntheses of the two.

1986

Ironic
Lyricism

I've read that you've translated poetry into Serbo-Croatian from Russian (Mandelstam, Esenin, and Tsvetaeva), French (including Baudelaire, Lautréamont, and Queneau) and Hungarian (Ady, Petöfi, and others). Do you see yourself as a translator in the broad sense of the word: someone who tries to acquaint Yugoslavs with other cultures?

I never had the desire to be a cultural ambassador or someone who translates for anything other than personal reasons. I've translated a lot of poetry from French, Hungarian, and Russian because I'm a frustrated poet. I began as a poet (though, fortunately, I never published a collection of my poetry), but finally I realized that the poetry I'd written was bad and that I could express myself better in prose, be it a novel, short story, or essay. But I'll always be extremely envious of poets and see myself as a failed poet. I'm one of those translators who fulfill their poetic impulses through their translations.

I also think—without being too didactic about it—that

the best literary training, including for those who want to write prose, is to translate poetry, to try to find equivalents in another language within, for example, the sonnet form. I should explain that when I say "translate poetry" I mean in the Yugoslav or Hungarian manner (as opposed to the French), in which you respect the rhyme and the rhythm. That's creative work.

You chose the poems you translated?

Almost always, I proposed the poets that I liked and found interesting. To this day, when I read a poem in a foreign language, I want to translate it immediately for my own benefit, to understand it better, to process it, to appropriate it.

You've described your very poetic prose in Garden, Ashes *as "intellectualized lyricism." What does that mean to you?*

So that lyricism in prose doesn't become lyrical in the everyday sense—sugary—it must be intellectual. What I often try to do in my prose is to express the feelings that gave rise to the writing, which are generally lyrical feelings, in a "philosophical" manner. And that is the definition of prose: irony against feelings.

In that book I had the problem of how to say very lyrical, maybe even sentimental, things about the more or less universal experience of childhood. The writing could save them by lending them a little irony. And I had to figure out how to express some of the very cruel events that affected this family so that they weren't filled with pathos. In short, I had to measure the salt, pepper, and sugar in that mixture. I tried to destroy the lyrical spell by putting big pieces of scrap metal, like that sewing machine, into the garden. Or the long list of nouns from a lexicon that should obliterate the perfume of plants in one section.

When you wrote this book, what writers were you thinking about as models for "intellectualized lyricism"?
I was thinking of certain Russian writers.

Pasternak?
I wasn't thinking of him (though it could apply to him as well) but of Babel, Pilnyak, and Olesha. What I've identified in myself can be found in twentieth-century Russian literature, rather than the nineteenth-century classics.

Did you study Russian literature in Belgrade?
I studied comparative literature at the University of Belgrade, which was an education in the great works of world literature (in the original or in translation, depending on which languages you knew), including Japanese and Chinese, Greek and Roman, French, American, and of course Russian works. And we read a lot of literary theory, which has remained with me. I'm still passionately interested in literary theory and have written a lot of articles and some books on it.

You know, when I finished Garden, Ashes, *I felt that I'd read a Faulknerian experiment in breaking down the reliability of a narrator: first the narrator sees his father as a god, later he's ashamed of him, and at the end the son seems almost as insane as his father.*
Yes, there's a shift in the point of view in this book,

which is more like the sequence of musical movements, because I don't like reading books in which there is just one movement—an allegro, for example. To a certain extent, the change of rhythm also required the shift in the point of view. After the glorification of the father came irony, which should demolish the apotheosis, because in literature nothing is safe from destruction. Everything is done so that it functions within the structure of the book, to serve the purposes of literature and not of reality.

And you've continued to experiment with point of view.

Yes, this book is part of a trilogy the order of which is: *Early Sorrows* (which has the subtitle *For Children and People of Refined Taste*); *Garden, Ashes*; and *Hourglass*. They are the three components of an autobiographical cycle I call the "family cycle." Someday I'd like to publish an edition of these books under that general title because they contain more or less the same events and the same central character, the father, from three points of view. In the first book, the father and the events are seen through the eyes of a boy, so there's a childish approach to the subject. Then the middle one—*Garden, Ashes*—mixes the two points of view, of a child and of a writer who identifies with the child. And in the third the narrator disappears and there's an objective narration—things are viewed as objectively as possible. Little by little, the novel describes the misunderstandings in an extended Jewish family in Hungary during the war, just before their destruction in 1944.

In *Hourglass*, there are four different accounts or movements that are intermingled. I felt again that one shouldn't see things from one point of view. For example, there are sections entitled "Notes of a Madman" which are written from the point of view of the main character, E.S., which was decoded in the preceding book as Eduard Scham. There are some sections which consist of straight description and others that describe the same reality but from different points of view.

The book is written in what I think is a rather simple manner: we witness the writing of a letter, and the letter at the end of the book clarifies the mosaic of events in the novel, for the principal character, for the reader, and for me, the writer. I don't want to encourage the reader to begin with the letter that's at the end because I think that would destroy the pleasure of slowly taking hold of the image. You enter this book by a strait and narrow gate and come into a dark and gloomy room, but by the end of the novel it's daylight, morning, and in front of you is the letter which will clarify everything that wasn't clear before. I consider this the only way to read the book, although I've heard that some readers wanted the letter at the beginning. And even some critics have reproached me for not putting the letter at the front. But I think that would contradict the logic of this piece of writing.

In A Tomb for Boris Davidovich *you also confused the reader—there, about what is historical fact and what is fiction.*

A reader likes to be told everything, but in that book I played around a bit, revealing things and fooling him at the same time. So one must be wary because I probably trick the reader most when I seem to confess something and when I offer the possibility of resolving a problem. There are true and false documents and one never knows which is true and which is false. The goal of every writer is to convince his reader that everything happened as he says, that this is truth, but in literature there is no truth. It's all my truth, the way I saw the events in books and documents, how I assimilated that world, how I spat it out. Whether it works as a book or not depends on the technique: was the reader duped or not, did I succeed in fooling him?

I gather that you drew on Karlo Štajner's Seven Thousand Days in Siberia *for much of the documentary material in that novel.*

A large number of the anecdotes which are expanded to become chapters of my novel are found in Karlo Štajner. That means he gave some facts—which I believe—and I began to think about what went on between two of his facts. He says, in a few sentences, that in the 1930s the French politician Edouard Herriot visited the Soviet camps and they put on a big show for him, according to a former KGB officer. He stops there, because that's enough for him, but I imagine pictures and write them down.

You wrote in your introduction to the French translation of Štajner's book that he found some anachronisms in your narrative and that you would correct them in the next edition.

I politely told him that I'd correct them, but in fact I didn't, because I think I was actually right. He was surprised when he read that one of my characters had worked in a wallpaper factory. He said, "But what are you saying there, young man? There was no wallpaper factory in Russia." Clearly, because his experience was mostly in [Soviet] concentration camps, he forgot that such a factory did exist. I had found a reference to a revolutionary who worked in a factory that produced wallpaper. There were things like that I checked and discovered I was right. On the other hand, there was a White Russian who read my book and said that it's not possible that a Jew could have been a schoolteacher in Russia before the Revolution. But I kept it anyway, because I had neither the time nor the inclination to check it. Some other readers made me doubt certain things and I changed them, but they were never important things.

Various critics have seen a relationship between your novels and those of Hermann Broch, Bruno Schulz, and Kafka. Do you think there is a Central European tradition—and, if so, how would you describe it?

I have nothing against the notion of Central Europe— on the contrary, I think that I am a Central European writer, according to my origins, especially my literary origins. It's very hard to define what being Central European means, but in my case there were three components. There's the fact that I'm half-Jewish, or Jewish, if you prefer; that I lived in both Hungary and Yugoslavia and that, growing up, I read in two languages and literatures; and that I encountered Western, Russian, and Jewish literature in this central area between Budapest, Vienna, Zagreb, Belgrade, etc. In terms of my education, I'm from this territory. If there's a different style and sensibility that sets me apart from Serbian or Yugoslav literature, one might call it this Central European complex. I find that I am a Central European writer to the core, but it's hard to define, beyond what I've said, what that means to me and where it comes from.

Do you think one can speak of a Central European literary tradition that is characterized by the grotesque and/or the lyrical?

Yes, the defining factor in the literature and thought of Central Europe in general is just that: ironic lyricism. Perhaps it's a combination of Slavic and Hungarian lyricism, with the ironic part, like a grain of salt, coming from the Jews.

Do you think that it's necessary for writers from so-called marginal areas like Yugoslavia or Hungary to gain legitimation in Paris? You said in an interview with La Quinzaine Littéraire* *that to be accepted as part of world culture one must gain attention and acquire recognition in Paris.*

I wasn't speaking there about those on the margins but about writers in general, including those from Latin America and the United States. You know that Faulkner became well known with Paris as his intermediary. And Latin American literature attained its high status through the mediation of Paris. I still think Paris—not France, but Paris—functions as a "big kitchen," as I said in that interview. There's always a lot of excitement, movement, arguments, in the universities and elsewhere. A lot of talk about books—books good and bad.

Do you consider Paris the world center of literary production?

No, I don't.

Just of literary reception and diffusion?

Exactly. It's a kind of permanent book fair where the

* From an interview conducted by Janine Matillon, *Le Quinzaine Littéraire*, January 16–31, 1980.

literary production of the world comes and makes itself known. It's like a fair in that people are hawking their wares. Although there's a large number of books produced, there's also a good chance of entering the market —few books go unnoticed. As you know, each newspaper has its literary pages. Almost every book will find an echo—large or small, pro or con—in the media. It doesn't mean that every book will get sold, but it will have a presence for one or two months at most, generally speaking.

Yes, I looked through a stack of your interviews and reviews at your French publisher, Gallimard. They'd be the envy of many serious writers in America who feel that they are writing in a void.

Of course, writers always feel that they are writing in a void. I feel that, too. Writers always want to see an immediate response to their products. That writers should be discontented is in the order of things.

Obviously, there can be misrepresentations and misperceptions of world literature at this fair. You once said that Westerners expect Eastern European writers to concern themselves with politics, not love.* Do you think there's pressure to conform to those expectations? In your works, I've noticed a conspicuous absence of the theme of erotic love, though not of the love between parent and child.

Europe sees us—the writers from the "other Europe" —as people who should always be involved in politics and write only about politics. They—the Americans, the Eu-

---

* From an article/interview in *Le Nouvel Observateur*, January 28–February 3, 1980.

ropeans, etc.—have the right to make use of all themes, including love, while they reserve only political questions for us. I'm fighting this because I don't want to be trapped in that ghetto.

But, on the other hand, it's true that when we from the "other Europe" write about metaphysical questions, we feel some discomfort, as if we had betrayed something more important. I seesaw all the time between those two feelings. When I write something that isn't political, I feel that I have been wasting my time on general questions, and when I write whatever I can about political questions, I think I've betrayed some important facets of life that are outside politics. As Krleža once said, "Politics is our destiny." I'd add that politics is our misfortune.

As for the absence of love in my books, it's true, except perhaps for *The Encyclopedia of the Dead*, which is a book about love and death, a completely metaphysical concept. I tried as much as possible to dispense with political questions but, nevertheless, the political is still there.

Perhaps this dichotomy is a historical fact and will be replaced by others, which may be equally insidious for writers, however.

I don't think so. I think there's an eternal opposition between *Homo poeticus* and *Homo politicus* which is very difficult to resolve. Every writer has to try to work out his own position, his own hierarchy of values. A writer whom I admire in this regard is Nabokov, who possessed a great deal of knowledge and experience but also had the self-control not to dive into politics because, while he could have accomplished something in the political sphere of his time, he would have destroyed his literariness, which he guarded. I think he's a good example of someone who knew how to gain distinction and was able to carry through on his knowledge.

Another good example is Joyce. You know the famous anecdote about his reaction to the news that the Second World War had broken out: he was mad because he had problems with his publisher and his readership. For him, his book was more important than the war. Although I might not be able to share his indignation and his indifference to the war, I understand what he meant and I can identify with the literary master at that moment.

Doesn't any straitjacket for literature, including the idea that literature must be "pure" and above politics, constitute a problem for writers? Those in the West may be constrained by the other side of the dichotomy: for us, the primary temptation—and sometimes the pressure—is to subscribe to the theory of art for art's sake. So I think that we must often argue for the stature of literature that concerns itself with political questions.

To that I'd say: Happy is the people that can avoid becoming politicized. And happy the writer who can resolve this problem of the political versus the metaphysical, the political versus the lyrical.

1986

Baroque and Truth

*When I look over the five books of yours published here in France, I see that the first three—*Early Sorrows; Garden, Ashes; *and* Hourglass—*deal with the same subject and form a sort of triptych.*

Yes, each serves as a correction of the one before it. *Early Sorrows* is written from the point of view of a child. *Garden, Ashes* brings the child's point of view together with the commentary of the narrator, a man of thirty, the two of them occasionally coexisting in the same sentence. In *Hourglass* I describe the same world from an objective, external point of view, the view of an author-God, omniscient and omnipresent, and the child appears only once, briefly, in the father's letter that ends the novel. It's as if we began with a sketch, moved on to a drawing, and came finally to the painting itself.

All three evoke a single traumatic reality: Central Europe laid waste by history, the Nazis, and anti-Semitic persecution. I can't help thinking of Adorno's question: Can literature be written after Auschwitz? Is the language of literature fit to deal with the height of barbarism?

Much as I find Adorno's question valid, I feel the issue is not so much moral as literary, or even stylistic: how to speak of such things without lapsing into banality. It was a real challenge. Hence the series of "corrections" I've just mentioned. Concentration camps and mass persecution make it hard for writers to deploy their favorite weapon: irony. How can you be ironic in the face of so tragic a subject?

Your answer seems to have been to approach it indirectly, centering your narrative on the person of the father, a character at once sublime and ridiculous, and not a little unbalanced. Is that what let you inject an element of humor?

You've hit the nail on the head, actually. The father character existed in reality just as I portrayed him; in fact, it was reality that enabled me to solve the problem. Being ironic about a mother is a difficult thing in literature; mothers tend to have only the most positive traits— they're beautiful, they're good . . . Think of Tolstoy. Fathers are more malleable.

Let me come back to history for a moment. In the two other books, A Tomb for Boris Davidovich *and* The Encyclopedia of the Dead, *you deal with Stalinism, the show trials, the Soviet camps, the fate of the victims. Yet I detect something different from Solzhenitsyn's grand fresco—an additional dimension, another variety of truth.*

Yes, there's a break in my work between the family cycle (the first three books) and what followed. I went on with my investigations, but substituting the experience of the century for my own personal experience. I felt it was wrong to take on fascism while ignoring Stalinism, especially as they have traits in common: the predominance of Jews in both Nazi and Soviet camps (*pace* Solzhenitsyn, who tends to bring in Jews only if they are camp guards).

More subliminally, however, my decision to write about such things involved a certain polemical, even ambivalent, relationship to Borges. Borges, as you know, wrote a work entitled *A Universal History of Infamy*, but it consists of rather lame stories. For me the true history of infamy is that of the camps. Particularly the Soviet camps, perhaps, because the Nazi ones were a logical consequence of the system, whereas in a country supposedly embodying progressive, humanistic ideals . . . Anyway, I attempted to treat it all as a kind of documentary à la Borges. I made abundant use of documents, in particular those provided by Karlo Štajner (who might be called a Yugoslav Solzhenitsyn). But while some of Štajner's testimonies provided the tissue for my stories, the descriptions were scanty enough to leave room for the imagination.

Of course I was writing in Yugoslavia, a country where certain features of Stalinism were present. I had seen and experienced them. While working on *A Tomb for Boris Davidovich*, I knew I'd have trouble getting it published. I was not mistaken.

To come back to my impression. They're not just documents. You move inside your characters and point out paradoxes, mind-boggling paradoxes. There are also elements of comedy at the very heart of the tragic. Isn't your sense of "comedy," the guileful

*way you stage things, isn't it in a way the essence of your art
as a writer?*

Yes. All my works contain a more or less metaphoric,
more or less hidden *ars poetica*. In *Early Sorrows*, for instance, it's the description of my mother's way of knitting.
The knitting sequences have a double meaning, both ref-
erential and indicative of my view of art.

It reaches a climax, I believe, in The Encyclopedia of the
Dead, *where practically every one of the nine stories may be
considered an allegory of the writing process.*

Definitely. Starting with the Simon Magus story. The
description I give of the authors' intentions in "The Encyclopedia of the Dead" is an indication of my own literary ideal: the ability to fashion the minutiae of life into
a mythical, eternal book, to reveal an immense, hidden
reality beneath a scant number of words . . . I find the
allegorical dimension of the work so plain, so obvious that
I'm amazed hardly anyone has noticed it.

*Isn't it a way of purposely clouding the issue, preventing the
reader from distinguishing between fact and fiction, document and
imagination?*

The dividing line between the two is also so obvious
to me that I take the greatest of pains to make the cross-
over as seamless as possible. I always begin with a document and subject it to what the Russian formalists called
ostranenie, defamiliarization, making what is familiar
strange. Otherwise, I'd be writing an essay. I'm incapable
of writing a book out of thin air. Even as a reader, I have
trouble with purely imaginative fiction: I see through its
artifices and am left with a mist or a void. The other

danger is to give the reader nothing but records or testimonials, to become a historian or memoirist. I gambol between the two perils.

That suggests a question about the relationship between writing and knowledge, what Barthes called "mathesis." Your stories often include "false knowledge," made-up references, and overtly parodic, Rabelaisian lists.

You're right to bring up Rabelais: he's still my favorite writer. You can learn more about the sixteenth century from his novels than from all the contemporary scientific and philosophical treatises put together. The only way to convey knowledge is in the form of parody. My definition of literature is an attempt at a global vision of reality and its simultaneous destruction.

Isn't there a connection here with a part of Jewish tradition? The sense of an interpretation constantly undergoing revision, a truth both necessary and never fully accessible, a union continually in need of renewal.

I would say I was Jewish more by fate than by culture. I knew the sufferings of a Jewish child during and after the war, though I am only half-Jewish and was baptized into the Orthodox Church at the age of four. But practically my entire family was exterminated, and that made me want to find out about Judaism, read up on the Jewish tradition. It's all quite bookish, if you like, though there's something willy-nilly Jewish in what I write, almost cabalistic at times.

What I had in mind was your way of inserting (especially in Hourglass*) a phrase like "That's never the way it is" and*

*intimating that whenever we think we've found something to hold
on to there's something else behind it.*

That's the one thing about me I think is essentially
Jewish. But that brings us back to my life: during the war
I had nothing to hold on to.

*If I were to draw up a literary family tree for you, it would
include Rabelais, Hermann Broch, Bruno Schulz, Borges. Are
you comfortable with them?*

Yes, perfectly, though I would add Isaac Babel and
Boris Pilnyak as well as two Yugoslav writers: Ivo Andrić
and Miroslav Krleža. In Part Three of *The Anatomy Lesson** I have listed all the writers who have meant something to me. It includes a number of poets, particularly
Russian and French. I myself began with poetry, but I'm
a bad poet. On the other hand, I've read and translated a
great deal of verse and still do. I believe reading and translating poetry to be useful training for writers of prose: it
teaches them to pare things down and, paradoxically, re-
strain their lyricism.

Would you agree that your work has a baroque quality to it?

Yes, there is a baroque dimension to what I write.
Flamboyantly baroque, you might say. But something
spare and severe as well. You might call it a conscious,
controlled baroque. I'm not satisfied with "verisimili-
tude," for example; I need to give the reader authentic
points of reference. I can't write without both authentic
data and literary devices. I tell my stories in the form of
documents, but turn the "document" into a form of fic-

---

* Included in this volume under the title "Schizopsychology," p. 52.

tion. (The eighteenth century did a lot of this sort of thing.) I even invent evidence. What I can't stand is the serialized or *feuilleton*-type fiction of the nineteenth and twentieth centuries and its hidden omniscient author who writes things like " 'I love you,' she told him, while thinking the opposite." As far as I'm concerned, an author must devise a stratagem to convince me of the truth of what I read; otherwise, I find the omniscience artificial, unnatural.

I'm incapable of writing to order. I can't write at all without two conditions: a subject that excites me, obsesses me, that I've got to get off my chest, and the appropriate form, a form I haven't used before. I keep feeling the need to change my style. I like starting from scratch each time.

1988

I Don't Believe in
a Writer's Fantasy

*What does Europe's historical and intellectual heritage mean for
your work as a writer?*

In my case, it is basically quite simple: I am first and
foremost a European writer. Yugoslavia, the country I
come from, belongs to Europe: its culture and literature
are European. In a narrower sense, however, I owe a great
deal to Central Europe: the Hungarian milieu I came to
know as a child, my knowledge of Hungarian and its literature, have had a decisive influence upon me. So, intellectually speaking, I've moved from Yugoslavia in the
direction of Central Europe. Which means, of course, that
the whole European heritage is my heritage—I am not
just myself. I see all European writers as having been
shaped by a threefold literary tradition: French, German,
and Russian.

*Your books are mainly set in the geographical and cultural space
of Central Europe proper, which stretches from Trieste to Cracow.*

European intellectuals have recently become unusually interested in the area. What lies behind this, in your opinion: nostalgia or a search for identity?

I dealt with the theme of Central Europe before it became fashionable—in my very first books, in fact. So it's pure chance that I'm included in the great movement to resuscitate the cultural and literary myth of "Central Europe." The reasons for the genesis of the myth lie primarily in the fact that a few years ago Western Europe suddenly became aware that an entire cultural tradition was leaving the historical stage, that its cultural heritage was in danger of dying out. The problem was mainly political in nature, because the gradual extinction of that cultural tradition stems above all from the continuing presence of the Soviet Union in the countries of Central Europe. On the other hand, the countries themselves have done precious little to stem the cultural decay: under Communist rule, the cultural and literary unity that had existed in the Austro-Hungarian monarchy fragmented all the more. Now things are looking up a little.

The fact that the process of cultural awakening began at all—first in Western Europe and only then, gradually, in the countries of Central Europe under Communist rule—is due to émigré writers from that region such as the Czech Milan Kundera, who now lives in Paris. But neither Kundera nor the others had any desire to unite this rediscovered cultural Europe politically. Their desire was to forge a cultural unity independent of political borders, to prove that an entity exists and that we are all heirs to the same culture, the same literature.

Reading your books A Tomb for Boris Davidovich *and* The Encyclopedia of the Dead *tempts one to characterize you as*

an encyclopedist of revolutionary utopias, like the ones who ap-
peared after 1789. What role does documentary material play in
your work?

I don't believe a writer has a right to give in to fantasy.
I don't believe in a writer's fantasy. Twentieth-century
literature has undergone a sea-change: literature is no
longer romantic, it *can* no longer be romantic in the historical sense of the word. For romanticism, fantasy was
the driving force of literature. After everything the history
of this century has dealt us, it is clear that fantasy, and
hence romanticism, has lost all its meaning. Modern history has created such authentic forms of reality that today's
writer has no choice but to give them artistic shape, to
"invent" them if need be: that is, to use authentic data as
raw material and endow them, through the imagination,
with new form.

Of course, it may be useful to use reality as a starting
point by introducing historical documents into the plot of
a book as proof, so to speak, of the authenticity of its
content. On the other hand, a historical document can
also serve to obfuscate: it can be used to *suggest* authenticity, it can lead readers to believe that everything they
read is authentic, whereas the author has something quite
different in mind. That's why good writers will want to
mix their ideas, invent a historical document without inventing history, forge a document, if you like, and thereby
re-identify historical reality through the imagination.

I see no value whatsoever in authentic documents, particularly with reference to the period you mention, which
dates from 1789—unless they are *testimonies*, such as those
of Solzhenitsyn, say, or Karlo Štajner, the author of the
shattering *Seven Thousand Days in Siberia*. Here the authenticity is so tangible that their books are of genuine

historical value. I have always found this period of history, crucial as it is to man's great betrayal, particularly interesting, which is why I undertook to document certain twentieth-century events in my own way; that is, to introduce false documents into my books and transform them, through the process of writing, through the imagination, into "real" ones. Had I used historical documents, I'd have been unlikely to have attained the degree of literary authenticity which—judging by their reviews—they convey in their present form.

What do you think is the cause of the twentieth century's utopian and ideological cravings?

With the disappearance of fascist/nationalist ideology and the ever faster crumbling of Marxist/Communist ideology, the situation has largely lost its edge. The world— it is now quite obvious—is turning to different forms of faith. This holds not only for Muslim states but for Catholic and Orthodox countries as well. Even Western, industrialized nations show a trend toward mysticism. People obviously need a total, totalitarian explanation of the world. Marxist ideology gave them a totalitarian explanation by attempting to define the mechanics of life and existence in terms of the class-struggle hypothesis. As people have come to realize that the Marxist explanation is inadequate, even incorrect, they have turned to a variety of faiths in the hope of finding an acceptable explanation. The nineteenth and twentieth centuries constitute the age of the great ideologies, the age when religious and mystic utopias were replaced by allegedly unified philosophical and political concepts. This project, which was a consequence of the Enlightenment, must now be regarded as a failure. We are turning again to mysticism and religious utopias.

Doesn't your literary struggle with the utopian and ideological forces of our age sometimes seem hopeless—even when, as you say, they are losing ground in the political arena?

From the viewpoint of eternity, everything is hopeless. But as Ionesco recently said, we have two great metaphysical mainstays: love and death; they are the stuff of our existence, and literature helps us to perceive them.

As for ideology, it is by definition outside poetry, outside literature. One of the great errors typical of the twentieth century is the interweaving, the tangling of literature with politics. Quite simply, it has been forced upon us writers. Even while writing a book like *A Tomb for Boris Davidovich*, I tried to make the best of a bad situation: poetry about a political subject, not politics. This does not mean I wish to betray the truth, of course; on the contrary, it is my testimony to the truth as I sought and found it in documents. When *A Tomb for Boris Davidovich* appeared, it was hailed far and wide as an eminently political book. But I claim that it is not a political book. My desire—and I thought that after Solzhenitsyn and everything else that has been written about the Soviet gulag and the history of the Russian Revolution it would be obvious—was to write a *poetic*, a *literary* work about familiar political facts. Nothing could have been further from the "political message" that many critics and readers think they found in the book.

One of your critics has labeled you a "Christian atheist." Would you agree?

My spirituality is gnostic in the sense I described in *The Encyclopedia of the Dead*. The essence of my spirituality is my dissatisfaction with this world. I am a sort of rebel against God's creation.

Your novel Hourglass *says at one point: "No religion is so perfect as to justify conversion. The only religion is the belief in God." Is this in fact your religious conviction?*

For a believer, for anyone seeking God, I feel there is no acceptable religion. That is why I don't feel there are any "good" or "bad," any "higher" or "lower," religions. In any case, God is not an idea that especially concerns me.

What about your Jewish heritage? What does it mean to you?

My Jewish heritage has brought me martyrdom. I lived in a family in which the Jewish religion was practically nonexistent. My mother practiced a form of Orthodoxy which, enriched as it was with her own ideas, might almost have been called paganism. Then at school during the war, through the good offices of a teacher who wanted to show me a bit of kindness during those hard times, I came to know Catholicism. But if I have suffered since childhood and all my life, it has been because people have seen me as a *Jew* and have behaved accordingly. Hungarian fascists and German Nazis discriminated against me as a Jew. When I became a writer, I began to write about Jews because I was familiar with their milieu. Sartre once said: "A Jew is not someone who is born a Jew; a Jew becomes a Jew because of others." In other words, I am a Jew insofar as others see me as one.

Some of the main characters in your books are Jewish intellectuals, Jewish revolutionaries, Jewish anarchists . . .

You're thinking of *A Tomb for Boris Davidovich*. It is a well-known fact that the Jewish intelligentsia and intellectuals of Central Europe played a leading role in the Russian Revolution. I see that as a great error on their part. They were obsessed with the illusion that it was possible—using Marx, of course—to build a just Communist society, more powerful than all national and nationalist leanings: put simply, an international society. Nowadays we see that the bankruptcy of the Soviet system and all other Marxist-socialist systems is caused in part by national feelings and nationalist impulses erupting and sweeping away Marxist ideology as if a dam had burst. This elemental feeling, this experience of belonging to one or another particular people, is especially strong among the nationalities of the Soviet Union.

Afterwards, under Stalin, the majority of the Russian Jewish revolutionaries were either shot or sent to rot their lives away in the gulag while the Jewish revolutionaries of Central Europe, unless they slipped out of Hitler's grasp in time, were consigned to the Nazi death camps. In this sense, I see little difference between the fate of Jewish intellectuals under Stalin and under Hitler. The Jewish characters in my book are there to document the similarity of the two systems.

The ideologies of this century have destroyed the lives of individuals by the hundreds of thousands, by the millions. Where do you see man's metaphysical choice?

My point of departure is that we know nothing. Metaphysics is a form of poetry in prose. Man is an unknown quantity. We don't know where we come from, where we are going, or why we exist. Religion, philosophy, and poetry (when I say poetry, I mean literature as a whole) attempt to supply us with answers to these questions. But neither religion nor philosophy nor poetry has the power to convince us with their answers: in all three cases we are dealing merely with the poetic metamorphoses of our quest for answers to such existential questions. Let's leave science aside for the moment—though even science, which many still think will sooner or later solve all our basic problems, is in the end only another poetic attempt to understand people and things.

We live in the unknown, as at the beginning of the world or at the beginning of human existence. Ideologies emerged as an attempt to fill this void: they are the simplest way for man to make himself believe that all the problems of existence have been overcome. This is the basis for their success—or rather, it was. Because nowadays, as I've said, we are turning back to religion, to myth.

In this context I would like to bring up another "point of faith," your faith in "the power of the book." What is its current status? What factors determine whether a book has "power"?

This is an issue I dealt with in *The Encyclopedia of the Dead*. Reading many books isn't dangerous; reading a *single* book is. People who have read just one book—be it the Bible, the Koran, or *Mein Kampf*—are the fiercest of fanatics in their religious or political beliefs. But there's also a problem if we look at the overall effect of literature on a person. Take the Germans: history tells us they're among the most cultured of peoples. They have world-famous writers, they're a nation of readers. But Goethe,

Schiller, Herder, Lessing, Heine, and Kant notwithstanding, Germany was the birthplace of Nazism, the death camps, the extermination of the Jews and other "inferior races." The fact that they read these authors, that they were educated in a spirit of humanism, was no obstacle to their descent into barbarity.

Also highly problematic is the theory that writers "do good" through their books. What "good" do they do? Poets and writers have repeatedly set forth humanistic ideas and ideals in their poems and novels—in Germany, in Russia, and elsewhere. They have written lies born of a revolutionary romanticism that fanned the flames of their imagination and enabled them to present them as truth.

I believe I can say of myself that I have never betrayed the true aims of humanity in any of my books. To avoid such a betrayal, writers aware of their responsibility must seek forms of artistic expression—be they autobiography or documentary—that enable them to get at the truth. They must beware of an imagination tainted with ideological or revolutionary faith.

You once spoke of your "poetic vision of the world," of your "sense of life as tragedy." Do you regard life as absurd, as one might assume from the destinies you write of in your books?

It isn't exactly stimulating for an individual to wallow in pessimism. But for me there's no denying the shadow of deep tragedy hanging over human life as a whole. As I've said: we don't know where we come from and know even less where we're going—from one void into another. In between, we have to struggle with the problems of existence, aging, illness, and a host of other things. The only consolation, one might say, is love. Even a tragic love offers consolation.

We writers are privileged in that we also have literature, artistic creation. It gives us the illusion that we are not living vain, meaningless lives, that we are making something substantial out of them. There may be other solutions, other illusions—religion, say. I myself would be the last to deny I have a pessimistic view of the world, and I know that something of this pessimism comes through in my books: despite their ironic tone, the reader often senses fear. This echo of pessimism, which frightens the weak, may be the reason my works are not as popular as those of certain other authors.

Despite your experience with the totalitarian ideologies and systems of our century, your books constitute a fierce defense of the unity and uniqueness of humankind. Would you agree that human individuality today, in both East and West, is threatened by collectivism?

My views on this question have changed a little over the last ten years. Let me explain my stance as clearly as possible. Any totalitarian regime destroys one's sense of humanity, and historical experience has taught us that people deprived of freedom develop substantially more radical, more selfish mechanisms to achieve and defend their interests than people living in a normally functioning liberal society. On the other hand, people forced to live under totalitarian rule often develop qualities and values they might not have developed without the pressure of such extreme conditions.

I know Soviet culture and literature quite well. Their example clearly shows how totalitarian pressures may, on the one hand, bring out the worst in human nature, the barbaric, and on the other hand inspire the most heroic. Nadezhda Mandelstam, the widow of the poet Osip Mandelstam, who was killed by Stalin's thugs, is a shining representative of many Russian poets, authors, and intellectuals who refused to betray their comrades—despite the terror that surrounded them and took their lives. And I wonder whether poetry, literature, and culture were not the factors that kept them from betrayal.

But I also wonder whether the very absence of poetry in both a metaphorical and a direct sense was not a precondition for Western man to find freedom, even at the cost of his soul.

In any case, it would be an oversimplification to claim that the oppressed are essentially evil and the free essentially good. Things are not like that. In fact, the same conditions may often have different effects on a person's character: we frequently find better human qualities among people under totalitarian Communist systems than among those from the free countries of Europe or the West in general. In other words, certain negative *and* positive qualities come fully to the fore only under conditions of extreme pressure. Perhaps literature can provide an answer to this problem, because if literature didn't show the peaks and abysses of human existence and the human psyche, the death of a child would be equivalent to the death of a sheep.

Of course, we must recognize the fact that particularly brutal forms of oppression deform and ultimately break a person's potential for humanity, but in some it also awakens undreamed-of powers of resistance and revolt that lead to an almost chemical transformation. That is why I view totalitarian systems as especially likely to bring out their subjects' positive and negative qualities.

Looking at history through the ages, do you see such a thing as human progress?

No, I don't. Looking back, we see that humanity has progressed in a technical and scientific sense, but not in terms of putting specific humanist concepts into practice. Here I totally agree with Arthur Koestler. The Yugoslav poet Miroslav Krleža once likened our twentieth century to an ape flying an airplane. This defines our situation perfectly. Our spiritual makeup has remained unchanged throughout recorded history. Take the postwar period, for instance. We have been confronted with the countless human victims of the Chinese Cultural Revolution, the horrors of the Vietnam War, the mass murders committed by Pol Pot's Khmer Rouge in Cambodia, a mad religious conflict in Northern Ireland, a brutal war in Afghanistan and a no less brutal war between Iran and Iraq, the bloody insanity of fundamentalism, and so on.

None of these contemporary conflicts differs in the slightest from wars in ancient or medieval times, except perhaps that "classic warfare" held fewer horrors for people: they were not exposed to the weapons of mass destruction we take for granted. We'd have to be extremely naïve to believe that people today are any different, any further along. In principle, I am convinced that history is the history of misfortune, that its worst aspects recur endlessly, over and over.

1989

Translators and Interviewers

INTERVIEWS

LIFE, LITERATURE

> *Interview conducted by Gabi Gleichmann, published in* Gradac, *1986*
>
> *Translated by Ralph Manheim*

IRONIC LYRICISM

> *Interview conducted by Karen Rosenberg, published in* Formations, *Vol. 5, 2, Summer/Fall 1986*

BAROQUE AND TRUTH

> *Interview conducted by Guy Scarpetta, published in* Art-Press, *April 1988*
>
> *Translated by Ralph Manheim*

I DON'T BELIEVE IN A WRITER'S FANTASY

> *Interview conducted by Adalbert Rief, published in* Universitas, *August 1989*
>
> *Translated by Francis Jones*

Ralph Manheim's translations were edited posthumously. Michael Henry Heim served as text editor for all the translations.